RECOLLECTIONS ON SRI CHINMOY

PART I

MAHIRUHA KLEIN

Copyright © 2022 Mahiruha Klein

No portion of this book may be reproduced in any form without express written permission from the publisher.

Cover art: Vilas Silverton

ISBN: 978-1-911319-43-6

First Edition went to press: 1 June 2022

www.ganapatipress.org

PREFACE

Around the turn of the millennium, Sri Chinmoy encouraged his disciples to start write inspiring news, articles and thoughts, related to the spiritual life for a new website called "Sri Chinmoy Inspiration Group". One of the most thoughtful and enthusiastic contributors was Mahiruha. He loves writing and for him, it is a real sadhana. Even 20 years after the initial burst of enthusiasm has waned for many, Mahiruha continues to share his thoughts, reminiscences and experiences reciting Sri Chinmoy's poetry. (though that is for another book!)

One thing I like about the writing of Mahiruha is that he combines a good sense of humour with thoughtful and direct prose. But, above all, Mahiruha is a real seeker, fascinated and inspired by the remarkable spiritual personality of our Guru, Sri Chinmoy. Mahiruha shares not only the beauty of being in the presence of Sri Chinmoy but also the ups and downs of his own spiritual life; he does this with humility, honesty and a spirit of self-giving to like minded seekers.

For those who did not live in New York, reading about functions with Sri Chinmoy was very inspiring. Even if you couldn't be there in person, Mahiruha's articles opened a little window into the experience of being in the presence of the Master.

This book is a collection of articles written by Mahiruha during Sri Chinmoy's time on earth. In part 2, there are also a few articles by other contributors to the Sri Chinmoy Inspiration Group.

— Tejvan Pettinger, Oxford, 4 May 2022.

ABOVE AND BEYOND

Above the ignorance of birth and death he is.
Above destruction-night he is.
Beyond the world of suspicion his life of integrity is.
Beyond question his miracle-faith is.
Above all earth-awards he is.
Above all Heaven-rewards he is.
Beyond the universal insecurity he is.
He embodies Eternity's Cry.
He reveals Infinity's Smile.
He manifests Immortality's Life.
Earth loves his heart of dedication.
Heaven adores his feet of protection.

- Sri Chinmoy [1]

---

1. Sri Chinmoy, *The Dance of Life*, part 3, *Aum Press*, Puerto Rico, 1973.

INTRODUCTION

By Mahiruha Klein

Sri Chinmoy was (and is!) my spiritual Teacher, and life-guide. I joined his path in the summer of 1997, having been an admirer from afar a few years prior to that. In reading these stories, you might find that I can sometimes seem to deify Sri Chinmoy, or put him on a pedestal. Sri Chinmoy himself, however, always claimed that Gurus like him are simply match-makers, who make an appointment between God and the spiritual seeker, and once he has brought the seeker to God, his job as a Guru is over.

I did feel the presence of God in my Master, and I also felt that my Master was identified with God at the deepest level. Joan Osborne asked, "What if God was one of us?" I believe that God does take a human incarnation from time to time, and that these incarnations do allow us to see and interact with God in a personal way. Christopher Isherwood preferred to describe Sri Ramakrishna as a "phenomenon", eschewing more contentious or controversial labels. I will also ascribe the term "phenomenon" to Sri Chinmoy, and just tell these stories as I experienced and remember them.

It is important to note that when writing about functions, this is all from my own words, it is not verbatim! It is from my memory, which may not be totally accurate! More than anything else, I am just trying to provide people with a sense as to what Guru was like. I think sharing even our half-remembered and distant memories of Guru is valuable. People in the future will want to know what it was like to be in the living presence of this great spiritual Master.

THE IMPORTANCE OF SATSANG:

Satsang is an old Indian term that refers to a community of seekers. People who believe in the same spiritual Master or tradition, often come together to celebrate their shared faith and way of life. These gatherings, and also all their daily interactions with each other are known as "satsang".

Our Guru, Sri Chinmoy, spent most of each year in his main spiritual community in Jamaica, New York. But every winter, for about two and a half months, he would travel to a different part of the world, usually either South America or East Asia, to spend some casual family time with his disciples. During these "Christmas Trip" retreats, Sri Chinmoy would often entertain his students with amusing stories, recollections of his days in India, and also anecdotes from the lives of other Masters. His students would organize fun tours to various notable sights in these countries, and also would put together races and other athletic events. At night, there would be plays, skits and very often musical performances. Underpinning all of these activities would be daily silent meditations, early in the morning, in the afternoon and also in the evening. It was a vacation, but also an opportunity for his students to grow spiritually.

Because of my work commitments in New York (where I was living at the time), I was unable to attend. But I did not feel deprived of my spiritual Master's inner presence. I lived just a few streets away from his modest home, in the little Briarwood neighborhood of Jamaica Queens. I could feel his spirituality reverberating through the streets and buildings, even in his absence.

I also felt that those of us who stayed behind appreciated each other more. We took added strength from our common bond, our commitment to this way of life. Jesus Christ said "When two or more of you are gathered in my name, I am among you."

I will never forget the weekly meditations we organized at Annam Brahma restaurant, a vegetarian establishment dedicated to Sri Chinmoy's philosophy. I felt Sri Chinmoy's presence there so strongly during the Christmas Trips. On Wednesday nights, many of us would cram into the restaurant, having pushed aside all the tables, and would meditate on a picture of our Guru in a high state of trance. Then, various male and female ensembles would present his spiritual music for us. Afterwards we would watch some film featuring Sri Chinmoy in meditation or during an interview. Then we would take Prasad (food that has been sanctified and offered to the Master's inner presence) and would go home, in a happy and blissful consciousness.

One of the main performers, "Hank", has been organizing soulful programs around Sri Chinmoy's poetry for forty years now. He's spent his whole life working in the Guru's restaurants, cutting vegetables and washing dishes. From spending so much time in our spiritual Master's flow, he has developed an other-worldly aura, in my view. He recites Sri Chinmoy's spiritual poetry for hours every day, and when I look at his eyes, I see nothing but celestial purity. I was happy that he usually organized the meditations in the Master's absence, because he made me feel that spiritual progress on this path is possible.

GUJURATI TEMPLE

For many years, Sri Chinmoy's New York-area disciples would meditate with the Guru in a public Elementary school located on Parsons Boulevard, called PS 86. Unfortunately, for a short period we lost the use of our beloved school. We tried to find a more satisfactory permanent indoor space to use, during the harsh winter months, and so we would meditate in different venues. Unfortunately, none of them met our needs.

We did meditate for a few months in a clean, bright Gujurati temple, located in Flushing Meadows. I had some nice experiences in that venue that I'd like to share.

While we were meditating in the hall, Sri Chinmoy would often circle around the room in his "chariot", a little motorized cart. His head would shake a little as he rode.

On this occasion, it must have been in the autumn of 2003, the Master circled around us two or three times and then paused to the right of stage to meditate on a big painting of a distinguished-looking Indian gentleman wearing a kurta and slacks. The gentleman depicted is an aged man, whose lips are tightly pursed together and whose dark eyes reflect courage and strength.

Sri Chinmoy then mounted the stage with great difficulty, due to an unfortunate arthritic condition, and meditated in silence for a few minutes. He gestured at the painting and said: "Vallabhai Patel – the Ironman of India."

At first I thought Mr. Patel was a great champion in weightlifting, but fortunately Sri Chinmoy clarified by telling us that Vallabhai Patel was the leader of the Indian Congress during British times, that he was extremely close to the freedom-fighter Netaji Subhas Chandra Bose, and that he achieved tremendous things towards the independence of India. Perhaps the painting in the hall is a famous image; it is certainly striking.

There was a painting of another famous Indian political figure to the left of the stage, but for some reason Sri Chinmoy did not meditate on or speak about this other figure.

Sri Chinmoy then asked for his harmonium. He sang many songs, accompanying himself. He began by singing a song dedicated to Sunil, a dear student of his who died two years previous. He also shared a charming story about Sunil. He said that he has taken a new incarnation in Russia.

I do not play any musical instruments, but I appreciated the fact that Sri Chinmoy gave of himself so completely and unreservedly as an artist – not just when performing for thousands of concertgoers, but even at these smaller gatherings with his students.

Later in the program, he spoke about how he is lifting much more weight than he did when he was on the "right" side of seventy. Now that he is on the "wrong" side of the fence, he is lifting much heavier weights. Continuing in this light vein, he remarked on how hard he struggles and cries to lose weight, but to no avail. He then kidded that perhaps the reason he sometimes lifts obese people is to make himself feel better about his own weight!

Towards the end of the program he noted that the Sri Chinmoy Bhajan Singers would be performing at a local Durga Puja, a celebration in honor of the Divine Mother.

He said that there are not one, but two Durga Pujas in India every year, at different times. I did not catch Sri Chinmoy's exact words, but he mentioned that Ramachandra, the first Indian Avatar, once prayed for Durga's help in his fight against Ravana. He said that it falls to the women in Indian families to read aloud from the Chandi, a sacred text dedicated to the Divine Mother, during the Durga Puja.

Recently, we lost one of our dearest spiritual sisters, "Lorraine" to cancer. Sri Chinmoy called up Lorraine's best friend and roommate and told her that he had helped Lorraine "immensely in her inner journey."

The woman he spoke to, "Kathleen" suffers from many physical disabilities. Even walking can be difficult for her. Sri Chinmoy was always concerned about her health, and gave her a lot of encouragement, advice and support. In spite of her challenges, she came to meditate with us on a regular basis, and was always kind and thoughtful to all. Her spiritual name meant, "I was born in the dawn-heart-garden of my Lord Supreme." A beautiful meaning.

In this case, I felt that our Guru helped Lorraine in her "inner journey" after death, just because of Lorraine's closeness and friendship with Kathleen. The Master's compassion cannot be bought, true, but again he can do many things for people who are truly dear and close to him.

Sri Chinmoy concluded the program by showing the video from an esraj concert he had given a few days prior at Niagara Falls.

A LUNAR ECLIPSE, AND A SISTER REMEMBERED

I am remembering another nice meditation we had at the Gujarati temple. I think it was in the late autumn of 2003.

On that occasion, the Sri Chinmoy Bhajan singers, an all-female ensemble dedicated to Sri Chinmoy's devotional Indian songs, performed for us for about one hour. We enjoyed a pretty hearty Indian meal and we also watched a video of Guru's morning weightlifting, with an emphasis on the original prayers he recited before performing each lift.

The Sri Chinmoy Bhajan Singers sang sacred songs not only to the traditional cosmic gods and goddesses, but also to Lily, Sri Chinmoy's late and beloved sister.

Sri Chinmoy told many cute and charming stories about his relatives, including one significant story connected with Lily's death. He wept bitterly when his sister died. Once, as he was grieving in private, sitting by himself in an airport lounge, her soul came to him and scolded him for crying for her physical. The soul, she explained to him, is the only real reality that we can claim. Sri Chinmoy responded to his sister by saying that the physical has its own supreme importance, and that was why he was crying.

I just want to quote the following paragraph about Lily from "My Brother Chitta," a book Sri Chinmoy wrote following his close brother Chitta's death in 1998:

"My sister Lily's nickname is Rani, which means "Queen." All her life, my sister has had the aura of a queen. When she walks, mixes with people, talks – in anything she does – she always maintains a very special kind of high dignity. She has a very soft oneness-heart also, but her queenly dignity is really something rare and unique." [1]

After the function many of us took our Indian meals outside to look at the lunar eclipse. The moon was a sullen, deep ochre, as if enveloped by heavy gauze. Interestingly, Sri Chinmoy's dhoti (spiritual garment) was the same deep orange or ochre color as the eclipsed moon.

***

The Gujarati Temple did not work out for us as a meeting venue, because it was too far. So, we began meditating at our open-air meditation space, called "Aspiration-Ground."

By then, autumn was quickly fading into winter. It was very cold, so the attendants had prepared a big tent for us all to meet in. The tent was well insulated and it wasn't cold inside it, but it was very crowded.

I often sat in the back at functions. But, one night, as there were no seats available at the back, I took one of the front-row seats. For some reason, none of the front row seats were taken. I was meditating very close to Sri Chinmoy.

[1] Sri Chinmoy, *My brother Chitta*, Agni Press, 1998

The gathering began with an opening meditation which lasted for at least fifteen minutes. Chela, Sri Chinmoy's dog, began barking for attention. The dog ran up to Guru while he was meditating. Sri Chinmoy was already in deep meditation, and his head moved slowly up and down and a distant smile played on his face. It was just interesting seeing a dog barking in front of a great spiritual Master as he was entering into his highest consciousness. I felt that Guru was aware of the dog from a higher level and he was smiling at the dog from a vantage point of compassion and oneness.

It was interesting, too, that an animal, which represents a "pre-human" consciousness, was interacting with a spiritual Master, who, while meditating, represents a "post-human" consciousness.

The dog calmed down, finally, and we had a long silent meditation. Afterwards, there was a film of Sri Chinmoy soulfully reciting prayers before weight-lifting. Here is one of them:

"My Supreme!
A seeker's
God-oneness-joy
Even death
Cannot take away.
My Supreme!" [2]

Sri Chinmoy then asked for one of his devotional "spoken-word" ensembles to perform. Their leader recited Sri Chinmoy's talk entitled, "The Short Cut, The Shorter Cut,

[2] *Unofficial. Currently unpublished prayer*

and the Shortest Cut" from the book "Everest Aspiration," accompanied by a group of highly skilled musicians.

It was a windy night. The tent shook and the flaps blew open a couple of times. But inside the tent all was calm and bright.

***

Most of the meditation programs held by Sri Chinmoy Centre are similar. They begin with a few minutes of silence, followed by various singing groups, and they often end with people telling whimsical or inspiring stories and the offering of prasad (blessed food).

Tonight it was very cold, even inside the insulated tent. Many of the local students kindly gave up their seats to the visitors. They stood outside and watched the performances.

Sri Chinmoy meditated in silence for a few minutes. Afterwards, he folded his hands and began singing the Invocation, his most sacred song. All of his disciples sing this song every day. We all joined him. Then he meditated for a few more minutes in silence.

After that, he called up an elderly Indian man. The two have been friends for nearly thirty years, and this gentleman plays regularly Guru's songs for us on the synthesizer. This gentleman was actually Guru's co-worker at the Indian consulate where he worked in the late '60s!

Next came performances by many singing groups. I liked Chidananda's group the best. This group consists of non-singers who sing Sri Chinmoy's "dictionary" songs: the first half of the song is a Bengali word, and the second half is its English equivalent. I think it's a group for people who are not "natural" or talented singers, but they practice a lot, and I think Sri Chinmoy said that they have made more progress than any of his other singing groups.

Interestingly enough, Sri Chinmoy said that it is great to be a genius, but a genius may not be aspiring to become better, or to improve. A genius may be satisfied with his achievement or standard. But if a non-genius constantly aspires to improve in his art, then that person may be pleasing God more.

I also like the fact that the Master always encouraged his disciples to advance in their own creative talents, whether in poetry, or music, or painting or anything else.

FUNCTIONS AT ASPIRATION-GROUND

Today was a special function at our outdoor meditation space. It looks like a cross between a tennis court and a Sri Lankan monastery!

On this occasion, Sri Chinmoy was taking questions from his singers.

I got there late, so I didn't hear all the questions and answers, but I did hear a few and I found it very inspiring.

One young woman asked if it was ok if we sang a song without knowing the meaning. Most of Sri Chinmoy's students do not speak Bengali, that beautiful language in which Sri Chinmoy so often writes and composes. Some of the songs may have sorrowful meanings, but the melodies are so beautiful that we get joy just by singing them. She was wondering if it is ok to sing certain songs with joy and enthusiasm if they really literally deal with loss and tragedy.

Sri Chinmoy gave a very interesting answer. He agreed that many of his songs express sorrow or helplessness. But sometimes out of sorrow and suffering we get joy. When someone dies and we cry for that person, we sometimes enlarge our own inner receptivity for higher light and higher truth. When we mourn we are comforted either by our loved ones or by God. He also said that, if someone dies, and we just use our higher philosophy, our spiritual wisdom: "Oh, God has taken back His son, God His taken back His daughter", then we can end up getting nothing from God! When we sincerely mourn for someone we loved, we do get blessings.

I like this idea a lot because I think it means that sorrow forces us to aspire, to dig deep within to find inner consolation.

Someone else asked Sri Chinmoy which is more important: to sing a song correctly, or to sing a song soulfully, even if we miss lots of notes. Sri Chinmoy responded that the soul of the song cares much more, infinitely more, for the soulfulness, the sincerity and the self-giving of the singer than for the correctness of the melody or the meter.

Another student asked Sri Chinmoy if there was any relationship between his soul-birds and his songs. As many people know, Sri Chinmoy has drawn millions upon millions of bird drawings, sketches and paintings in many media.

Our spiritual Guru answered by saying that his soul-birds go up, high, higher, highest, while his songs spread all around. He then told an interesting story to explain the nature of his songs.

Once a spiritual Master in India gave a special mantra to a particular seeker and told him to keep it secret. If the seeker told anyone the mantra, the Master explained, then the mantra would lose all its power and it would be useless to him. The seeker replied that he didn't want his mantra for his personal benefit alone; he wanted everyone to be able to get light from his mantra. So he ran to the nearest mountain, climbed all the way up and screamed the mantra at the top of his lungs. Many people heard him and they began to practice this mantra and they benefited.

In the same way, when we sing spiritual songs soulfully we offer light and love to the whole world, to all humanity. But we have to sing soulfully and sincerely. I am no singer, but I do feel Sri Chinmoy's songs have a natural divinity, a divine touch.

***

Tonight's meditation began with Sri Chinmoy circling quietly around the room in his motorized "chariot" which looks like a go-cart. It's the kind of vehicle a child might treasure. I happened to have been sitting in an aisle seat, so that I could see Sri Chinmoy very clearly. His face reflected serenity.

As I meditated in silence, I felt myself letting go of all the worries, anxieties and frustrations which have been plaguing me recently. I felt like a child again, too.

Sri Chinmoy said once that all true spiritual Masters teach meditation in silence. That reminds me of a quote from Taoism. I'll have to paraphrase it, but I think it goes something like "If a student asks a question about the Tao, and the teacher answers it, then neither of them know anything about the Tao."

After the opening meditation, Sri Chinmoy offered a spiritual name to one young woman. She is a photographer and a musician.

After that, a male aphorism group offered a presentation of Sri Chinmoy's poetry and vocal and instrumental music. They are led by my friend Satyajit who has devoted his whole life to the Master's devotional poems and songs. I like Satyajit's recitations because he brings out the natural cadences in Guru's writings. He brings the writings to life.

After that, my friend Trishatur told the inspiring story of

his efforts to establish a meditation group in Cambodia. He said that when he went to a secondary school in a remote village, that the students all listened so attentively to him, and practiced the breathing and chanting exercises with utmost zealousness. He contrasted the poverty that they live in with their eagerness for spiritual wisdom.

He also remarked that spirituality isn't just meditating in front of your shrine. You can be shopping or just walking down the street, but if you're in a good frame of mind or in a cheerful, soulful consciousness, people will receive some inspiration from you. He connected this with the remarkable success he encountered in Cambodia; and the seekers who responded to his lectures with sincere interest.

Ranjit and Unmesh performed next on their Indian instruments. They danced like baouls (Indian mendicant-singers) while they played their instruments. Given that their instruments were big and heavy it was definitely fun to watch! For the uninitiated, Ranjit and Unmesh are two brothers who have studied with Sri Chinmoy for many years. They often travel to holy places in India and show fascinating slide shows of their journeys (and foibles!). They perform pieces that were dear to Sri Ramakrishna or pieces that were popular with the Brahmo Samaj (an Indian philosophical movement of the 19th Century). These songs are unfamiliar to me, and as I don't speak Bengali, I can't understand them. They sound a bit like rustic American folk music. The fact that the brothers sway back and forth as they sing makes the comparison seem more obvious.

The meditation concluded with a big, sugary prasad (as usual!). Sri Chinmoy tossed a chocolate sweet to each person as he or she came up for prasad. After everyone had taken prasad, he threw handfuls of candy into the men's section and women's section, alternating between them. We men maintained some poise and dignity as we tried to catch the candy. The women laughed a lot.

***

When I arrived at the meditation tonight, Sri Chinmoy was already sitting in his armchair, on the little stage. The entire room was so silent; we all meditated and meditated together for a long time. He asked the women, then the men, to walk around the front of the room where some of his most recent bird drawings and sketches were displayed.

From meditating with Sri Chinmoy I have become more acquainted with the concept of spiritual silence. I had a philosophy Professor in College who, earlier in his life, lived as a monk and kept a four year vow of silence in a monastery in upstate New York. I've never understood why he did that, but from my time with my own teacher, I think I may understand better what silence is.

After we meditated, Sri Chinmoy asked one of his assistants to play a tape which featured some arrangements of his music that a well-known Russian composer made. I have never heard Sri Chinmoy's music presented in the Western classical mode before. I've studied and enjoyed classical music all my life, so it was a rare treat for me to hear it.

I don't cry. Ever. Men, in general, Do Not Cry. Isn't that a rule? But, I'll say that after hearing one particular arrangement that tears flowed down my face freely. I looked around and I saw that almost everyone, women and men, were also similarly moved. I hope these arrangements become widely available soon!

After that, he asked Ongkar's daughter and his wife to come on stage and to display a beautiful collage of photographs, drawn from Ongkar's life. I don't know how else to express this, but while they were talking about Ongkar, I felt the entire room was filled with the sweetness that was such a true and integral part of the man's personality. I will never forget him.

Sri Chinmoy then offered a special chocolate candy prasad in honor of Ongkar. We stood in line and he offered the candy to us individually.

At the end of the evening, Sri Chinmoy asked for a few more of this Russian composer's arrangements to be played. He told us afterwards that he was extremely, extremely pleased with these arrangements, and that they were unique in every sense of the term. He said he doesn't know anything about classical music, but that his heart has ears, and that these arrangements would remain unparalleled. He said something like, and I am sorry to paraphrase, that nobody in the near future would create arrangements so beautiful. He then paused, and said that even in the distant future he does not see anyone matching this achievement.

***

Tonight was our weekly Wednesday night meditation meeting. I got there a little early, took my seat in the bleachers under the old, winding trees and the stars and read selections to myself from Sri Chinmoy's books.

I enjoy reading and meditating by myself before the start of the meditation. Interestingly enough, I often feel Sri Chinmoy's consciousness pervading the amphitheater even before he comes physically.

Tonight, when Sri Chinmoy arrived, he circled the tennis court in his motorized "chariot". His face radiated joy, and also a childlike purity. I once saw a picture of Sri Chinmoy riding an old fashioned locomotive and smiling from ear to ear like a little kid. I guess he likes his go carts partly because they bring out the child in him.

Almost all of the visitors are gone now, and Aspiration-Ground seems so empty. I feel that whenever people meditate and pray together sincerely, that vibration or force goes out into the world and becomes part of humanity's consciousness. During Celebrations, I really feel that our large-scale collective meditations are useful to the world. They have to be.

Sri Chinmoy's old friend, Ram, performed some of his favorite songs of Sri Chinmoy's on the harmonium. I think Mr. Ramamoorthy helped Guru a lot when he first came to America, so the Master remembers him and honors him by having him play for us every week. Gratitude and remembrance.

All of the local groups performed soulfully. I particularly enjoyed the performance of one of our great flautists, who interpreted a couple of Sri Chinmoy's songs dedicated to the Lord Buddha. Very simple songs, they yet made me feel I was rising to a more refined state of mind.

A Ukrainian women's trio performed on their national

instruments, whose names escape me. Excellent.

Of course, Ranjit and Unmesh, in the garb of Baouls (religious mendicants), and playing ektars (single stringed instruments used to accompany devotional singing), shuffled across the court singing the songs that the Brahmo Samaj and also Sri Ramakrishna used to sing. Once again, you have to be there.

Sri Chinmoy meditated on the mother of one of his students, towards the end of the program. They meditated together for a long time, and then he garlanded her with a beautiful flower garland.

***

Tonight the meditation started a little earlier, at six-thirty, rather than at eight. The reason was that Sri Chinmoy was given an honorary degree from a distinguished Bangladeshi University. The Chancellor of the University flew all the way from Bangladesh to confer this honor upon Sri Chinmoy.

Sri Chinmoy performed on the esraj for a few minutes; and then he meditated in silence with the guests from the University. After that, the Chancellor spoke about the history of the University and presented Sri Chinmoy with the honorary degree. The gentleman spoke at length about Sri Chinmoy's tireless efforts towards world peace, and in particular his Oneness-Heart-Tears-And-Smiles programme which offers humanitarian aid to the needy all over the world.

Sri Chinmoy, on accepting the award, spoke about how he lives in America, but his heart remains in Bangladesh.

And he reminisced about his native village, Shakpura, and the nearby city, Chittagong, and he said that he treasures his happy memories of his childhood there. He also said that he is offering his heart's gratitude-tears to his mother and father and also to his brothers and sisters, who are now in Heaven. Maybe Sri Chinmoy wanted to invoke their memory on this special occasion.

After that, Sri Chinmoy lifted the Chancellor and offered his deepest gratitude to the man for offering him this great honour.

A devotional poetry group, consisting of Guru's students, recited quite a few poems, with musical accompaniment. After their performance, Sri Chinmoy read out some poems by a Bengali writer of the last century whose name I don't recall. He then also spoke about a famous Bengali novelist, Sarat Chandra, who was really supremely great. He said that Sarat Chandra and Rabindranath Tagore were great rivals. He also remarked that Sarat Chandra had a dog which was uglier than the ugliest and, at the same time, ferocious. Sarat Chandra had many literary admirers, who were themselves writers of the highest order. They would come to his house and the dog would snarl and bite them. But they used to offer the dog so much love. And when the dog died, Sarat Chandra cried as if his own mother or father had died. And his friends and literary admirers wrote poems and stories about this cur and read them out at its funeral!

Today, September 27, was our late and beloved Jagatarini's birthday. Jagatarini was a disciple of Sri Chinmoy who hailed from Yugoslavia, but who relocated to Russia, and learned Russian, to establish the Master's mission in that country.

She served Guru for years and years, tirelelssly.

There was a big photograph of Jagatarini beside Sri Chinmoy's chair. She was smiling in the photograph, wearing a beautiful garland of marigolds. He spoke about her great service to the spiritual cause, and how her immense soul had come to bless us all. The singers sang beautiful songs in her memory. I still miss her very much, and will always cherish her incredible strength and sincere affection.

Today is also Sri Chinmoy's twenty-third cello anniversary! What a remarkable anniversary indeed. Many, many congratulations to Sri Chinmoy on this great occasion.

I love and treasure his immortal cello recording from 27 September 1996, "The Promise of a New Dawn."

MAHIRUHA KLEIN

FUNCTION REPORT: Q & A WITH GURU

I asked Sri Chinmoy if he would explain the essence or the quintessence of Beethoven, as opposed to the essence of Bach. I explained to him that both composers have inspired me tremendously in my life, but I was wondering if he could explain how two such great composers could be so different. I also asked Sri Chinmoy if spiritual seekers could make progress by listening to these two composers.

Sri Chinmoy began his response with a rhetorical question, asking if anyone in the world knew less about these things than he does. He paused for a few seconds and then added, "My mind does not understand, but my heart appreciates it [their music]".

He said that when he listens to Beethoven he feels that his music is like a fully blossomed tree: branches, leaves, flowers, fruits. But then thunder comes and the tree is shaking – but the tree is not coming apart. And all the branches are moving, moving, moving – each branch is moving in a different way, but the branches are not fighting.

He explained this analogy by saying that in Beethoven there is unity and complexity at the same time – like a fully blossomed tree. The thunder, which shakes the tree, is Beethoven's unparalleled musical capacity. And the branches are moving, each branch moves in its own way, but they are not in conflict with each other. In other words, inside Beethoven's complexity he was able to preserve unity. With most composers and artists, once complexity comes, unity goes away. But Beethoven was able to keep both at the same time.

He also said that because Beethoven was deaf, he had to get the music from his inner eye, his third eye. Once he became deaf, he heard and received the music through his third eye.

He then spoke about Bach. He said that prayer-life was a very important part of Bach's personality, and that he appreciates Bach spiritual depth. He said that he does not find simplicity in Beethoven's music, but that Bach's work is simple and yet very, very deep. I think he said that we can dive deep, deep, deep into Bach's music. I also think he said that inside Bach's music there are prayers, that he imbued his music with a prayerful consciousness.

He then said that if we use our heart we will say that oneness is the only reality, and that we don't have to judge these two composers, or say which one we like better. But if we are completely honest with ourselves then immediately we will know of whom we are most fond.

He then said that Beethoven is like a rose, and Bach is like a lotus. And that a garden has so many flowers, and each flower is indispensable to the glory and beauty of the whole garden, but the gardener definitely knows which flower he likes most.

He said that a mother has ten children and she will say that she loves all her children equally but that this is a sheer lie, an utter lie. She knows whether she likes this one or that one or that one. So, in his case also, Guru said, inwardly and outwardly, he loves the music of Bach more than Beethoven, and that if he has to choose between the rose and the lotus then outwardly, to avoid problems, he will say that he loves both equally, but in the depths of his heart, he knows he has chosen lotus. He put his hand on his heart chakra when he said that last part.

After a long pause he commented that Bach and Beethoven are like a flute and a drum – again so often a flute can play the role of a drum, and a drum can play the role of a flute. But one is flute consciousness, and the other is drum consciousness.

I enjoyed Sri Chinmoy's kind and expansive answer to my question as I also love Bach most. I'm not putting down Beethoven at all, on the contrary! I'm just saying that Bach's music, especially his Passion music, contains some of the most haunting devotional feeling I have heard anywhere. It seems to come from another world entirely. I think any seeker from any path would benefit from listening to Bach.

A CHANCE ENCOUNTER

One afternoon, perhaps seven or eight years ago, I was working at The Oneness-Fountain-Heart Restaurant, behind the cash register. A respectable-looking middle-aged gentleman came in and looked around the restaurant, gazing appreciatively at our original Jharna-Kalas, and also at the television monitor which showed some of Sri Chinmoy's recent inspirational activities. Finally he picked out two cassette tapes from the display and approached the counter.

As I was ringing him up, I noticed that he looked familiar, but I couldn't put my finger on it. I asked him if we had met before. He responded by asking me how long I had been a disciple. When I told him, he explained to me that he left the Centre just a few years after I came. Probably I recognized him from one of my early Celebrations.

He spoke a beautiful, formal kind of English, and I asked him which part of England he came from. I was embarrassed when he told me that actually he came from Australia! (Not, mind you, that there's anything wrong with being Australian; it's just that I take some ill-founded pride in my accent-recognition ability.) He added that he had grown up speaking very, very proper English at home, which was why people often thought he was British. He is now an international businessman, and he explained to me that he was driving across the United States for his company. He wanted the tapes so that he could hear Guru's voice as he drove around America.

I thanked him for stopping by and he gave me a sweet smile. As he was leaving, I reflected on the fact that not all people who leave a spiritual group take an apostate stance. In fact, I remember how Guru once said that some of the so-called "former-disciples" are actually closer than the closest to his heart!

I heard from a friend that Guru once remarked that some of the people who left long ago actually continue to make spiritual progress because they remember what they received from Guru, and they treasure those experiences in their hearts.

I can think of no better way to spend my time than to remember my own experiences with Guru, and the love and compassion he showered on us so magnanimously.

ANCEDOTES

Sri Chinmoy was always interesting to be around. At functions, sometimes he would just sit in his chair, and hum to himself, or draw, or practice some of his favorite songs. But I never felt bored in his presence. I found his aura, his presence, endlessly fascinating. In his quiet moments, he still exuded a heavenly peace and serenity that lifted people up to a different place. Maybe that's why Sri Chinmoy always said, that for a God-realised Soul, manifestation was automatic. The moment you stand in the presence of a truly realized spiritual Master, you feel what he has and what he inwardly is: peace, purity and happiness in infinite measure.

***

I think Guru told this story in the summer of 2002, at an evening function. He prefaced the story by saying that he, like all spiritual Masters, has a human aspect and a divine aspect.

He then went on to tell an incident that occurred that very morning. He was returning to his house, unaccompanied, in his little car (it was red, right?) and, as he entered the driveway, he saw an Indian man rooting through his garbage cans. He said that man was dark "like me". He honked the horn to drive the man away. At that very moment, the divinity in him reprimanded him. I think he even said that it "struck" him. It said, "How can you be so cruel? How can you be so heartless? The things that you are discarding this man is cherishing!"

Then he slowly drove into the driveway, and as he passed the other man, he leaned out of the window and gave him the broadest smile, while also inwardly begging him for forgiveness.

Guru concluded by saying that whenever we do anything wrong we should immediately try our utmost to rectify it.

***

As you know, Guru had perhaps a half dozen people who used to take him on daily drives around Queens. On those drives, Guru would usually meditate in silence. Sometimes he would do japa (soulful chanting).

Databir drove Guru frequently, and he told me about a special experience he had with Guru in the late Seventies:

One morning, Databir drove Guru by the Thomas Edison soccer field in Jamaica, Queens, where our annual Sports Day is held. There, they saw perhaps fifteen or twenty female students of Sri Chinmoy playing softball. Databir told me that the women weren't aware of Guru's presence, so they weren't in a particularly soulful or "spiritual" consciousness. They were just playing softball, badly and unprofessionally, and laughing and having fun. Databir and Guru watched them playing for a few minutes. Then Guru turned to Databir and said, "They will never know how many diseases this prevents."

***

Once somebody gave Guru incorrect information, telling him that I went to Princeton. I did not go to Princeton. I went to a nice college. But it was not Princeton.

From that day on, Guru was convinced that I really had gone to Princeton. Even when I told him that no, I had not actually gone there, I think he still believed that I actually attended that most venerable ivy-covered institution.

My grades and SAT scores would have made a Princeton admissions counselor laugh!

But all this goes to show that Guru did not see us as we were, but rather as we wish we were. He saw me at my very, very best – the absolute ideal me that I may never reach but is still buried somewhere deep inside my heart.

***

In late December of 2007, I was employed at Pole-Vision-Life-Strength Health Foods on Union Turnpike. I worked at the cash register and also did some stocking. Once I was working at the register with another employee when a middle-aged Black man entered the store.

He bought some ginger beers and chewy k-rations (sorry, that's my name for the ultra-salty and tough shoe-leather snack that's supposed to be imitation beef jerky). After he paid, he told us that, in the Seventies and early Eighties, he used to attend the Master's public meditation functions at Hillcrest high school in Jamaica.

He described how Guru's eyes used to go back and forth at lightning speed. As he was describing Guru's eye movements he just bubbled over with excitement.

"He was the most fantastic soul on the planet!" he concluded, before walking out.

My friend and I just looked at each other.

Just how many lives did Guru touch? Who knows what kinds of inner experiences people got from Guru?

I think Guru said once that some people who maybe only saw Guru once make faster progress than even his long-time students do, because they treasure what they got from Guru. They remember their experiences.

From the moment I met Sri Chinmoy, I felt certain that I wanted to be his disciple. My Centre leader, however, felt that it might be good for me to meditate with him a few times, as a seeker, before making a commitment to his path.

As a seeker, I had the opportunity to meditate with Sri Chinmoy every Friday, at the public meditations at PS 86. I would go up on stage with the other seekers and sit in front of the Master, not even four feet away, and meditate. To be more precise, I would just look at Sri Chinmoy's face as he entered into a higher consciousness. It's a little difficult to describe in words, but when he meditated, his whole face radiated the calm, tranquil and innocent joy of a little child. I mean, his eyes would be flickering and moving from side to side at tremendous speed, and the most distant smile would play upon his lips. The joy that he radiated was something of the most incredible purity and beauty. When I saw him meditating, I felt that I was in the immediate presence of the Divine.

Also, the whole consciousness of the hall would change dramatically. I mean PS 86 is a public elementary school in a pretty rough neighborhood in Queens. But after the Friday night meditations, the whole room became a sacred temple, full of purity and sweetness and peace. I will never forget those meditations. I am happy that I did not become a student of his immediately, as that gave me an opportunity to meditate with the seekers, and thus to sit close to him and to observe him in deep trance. That was the privilege of a lifetime.

"A true spiritual Master must shoulder
The countless responsibilities
Of his spiritual family.
But still he remains
In a childlike consciousness
To fill his seeker-children
With the joy and delight
Of God the eternal Child."[3]

***

An elderly disciple couple from the West Coast told me about this experience with Guru. In the early Seventies, they drove all the way across the country to attend a Joy Day in New York. After the Joy Day, Guru granted them a short interview and asked them how they had been. The

[3] *Sri Chinmoy, Ten Thousand Flower-Flames, part 77, Agni Press, 1983)*

wife answered that they had been doing well, but that she had been suffering from an excruciating dental condition. She mentioned that her parents had offered to loan her the money, two hundred dollars, to get the necessary corrective procedure.

Guru was flabbergasted! He simply could not understand how a parent could even think about loaning money to a child. He left the room in a huff and promptly came back with four hundred dollars which he handed to the wife.

"I am your divine father," he said, "whom you do not have to pay back!"

***

Once, one of Sri Chinmoy's students, who works at the UN, took a bathroom break and decided to take the opportunity to sing some of the Master's songs. Afterwards, she was approached by another woman in the hallway. "I heard you singing in the washroom. Were you singing in Yiddish?"

The lady got a big kick out of that, as so many of her friends in the Sri Chinmoy Centre are Jewish!

On the same theme, another young woman who works at the United Nations was once invited by one of her colleagues to join her for a special Shabbos (Sabbath) meal, offered by the local Chassidic community. A great Rebbe, visiting from overseas, would be presiding. After the meal, the Rebbe asked everyone present to sing a spiritual song. It didn't have to be from the Jewish tradition. As she did not know any Jewish or

Hebrew songs, she sang one of Guru's Bengali songs, maybe "Ar Katokal Kandbo Mago." The Rebbe was impressed by it, and said that that song expressed the longing of the soul for the "Eyn Sof" (the Endless One).

***

For some reason, I have been thinking of the brilliant-colored garments that Guru used to wear at his public meditations. I went to college in Trenton, New Jersey, and would often take the three and a half hour trek up to Queens every Friday to attend public meetings with the Master. I just remember the beautiful pink, purple, blue and white dhotis he used to wear. For some reason, I was most affected when he would wear just plain white. I always had the best meditations when he would wear simple white. But no matter which color he wore, he always exuded this humility, grace and purity.

I think Guru said that when he wears white, just simple white, that he sees that he is simply oozing Compassion. I do not have the exact quote and if somebody can supply it, I will be grateful. I just remember Guru saying that white is not the color for Compassion, but for purity, for the Divine Mother, but that when he wears white, Compassion just flows from him.

MAHIRUHA KLEIN

MEMORIES OF GURU

I remember with great fondness some of the spiritual talks that Guru gave us at PS 86 or Aspiration-Ground. Alas, I very rarely took notes. But I remember some things.

I remember after the public part of a Friday night meditation had concluded, Guru told us that he would love us forever and forever and forever. He said that in the distant future, in our future incarnations our inner being may come to the fore and give us the message of Guru's love for us. But, he said, our outer minds will find it so difficult to believe it, that anyone could love us so dearly, so completely. But, he said, emphatically, he will always, always love us.

Some years later, I remember Guru gave another talk at PS 86. He said that we should try to resurrect good habits from our past. The past is dust, true, but if we did good things in the past, inspiring, aspirational activities that gave us joy, then we can try to resurrect those good habits. For example, maybe we wrote "Supreme" twenty-seven times every day in our diary, or maybe we played tennis with other disciples. If we can just do the good things that gave us joy, then that can really help us in our spiritual life.

Once a group of women singers from Florida sang some of Guru's songs during Celebrations. Guru liked their performance a lot. He commented that some singers are born, while others are made. He said that these singers in front of him were ʽmade' singers. In other words, they practised and practised and worked very hard to acquire their facility in singing. He said that through practice and diligence we can become poets or artists or musicians or whatever we want. He was pleased with their tenacity and determination to become singers.

TWO SISTERS

In the early 1970's, two sisters became disciples of Sri Chinmoy, and developed a very close spiritual connection with the Master. One of them had practiced Zen most seriously before joining our path. Unfortunately, this sister gradually became mentally incapacitated and had to enter an assisted living facility, where she stayed for many years. In the autumn of 2006, the sister who remained as an "official" disciple brought her to a Wednesday night meditation with the Master. I understand that, due to this lady's condition, she had not visited the Guru for quite a few years, maybe even decades. She was completely withdrawn and mute, unable to communicate in any way.

At the end of the meditation, her sister took her by the shoulder and guided her through the Prasad line, step by step. When it was their turn to stand in front of the Master, Sri Chinmoy stopped the line and called the catatonic woman's name with great enthusiasm and affection: "Maitreyi!" Her sister gently helped her to stand a little closer to the Guru. Then, Sri Chinmoy smiled, grinning almost from ear to ear, and it seemed he was gazing into a vast, unguessable distance. His eyes shifted back and forth a number of times, and then he folded his hands and bowed to her. The woman seemed to bow back ever so slightly.

I got the impression from looking at Guru's face that he was identifying himself with this disciple of his. Wherever she was, he was able to make contact at the deepest level and to offer his blessingful love to her. Maybe that says something about the Guru's promise, that he will never leave us. No matter what happens in our inner or outer lives, he will never forsake us.

MAHIRUHA KLEIN

GURU'S VISIT TO CHICAGO, 3 AUGUST 2002

It's been about ten years since Guru's momentous visit to the Windy City to offer his wonderful concert, "Prayerful Music with Sri Chinmoy", at the Palmer House Hilton.

My memory is leaky, but I remember some inspiring things. I remember flyering in downtown Chicago and giving a flyer to a big, stocky Black man. He saw Guru's face and said, "Isn't he the guy who does all the weightlifting?" I smiled and said yes. I was always really gratified when people recognized Guru and knew about some of his inspiring activities.

I remember the morning of the Concert, Guru met with Sukhukee at our restaurant. Her name was Ida at that time, but that morning, Guru meditated on her, created a beautiful Jharna Kala in her honor and offered her the spiritual name "Sukhukee – Darling of the Divine Mother." At the bottom of the painting he wrote, "Your Eternity's Brother, Chinmoy"

Sukhukee was in her mid-eighties at the time. She actually knew Guru from the Sri Aurobindo Ashram, where she stayed in the guest house. During her first visit to the Ashram, she visited Nolini-Da, the Secretary to Sri Aurobindo and great savant in his own right. Guru was working as Nolini's personal assistant at that time. When she walked into Nolini's foyer, she saw Guru working at the desk and looked into his eyes. Then, when she returned to America, she wrote a letter to the Ashram saying that she had seen the most beautiful light in Guru's eyes.

Guru is so funny! While he was meeting with Sukhuhee at the restaurant he reminded her of that letter she wrote to the Ashram and then remarked, "But now my eyes have lost all their light".

Guru had said some years previous to this that Sukhukee was the only person in the Ashram who supported him fully in his wish to come to America.

The concert itself was simply splendid. I was able to get almost a front-row seat because I had helped to publicise the event. The closing meditation, where Guru held a portrait of Swami Vivekananda to his heart, was very powerful.

The next day there was a special "Lifting Up the World With a Oneness-Heart" ceremony, held in the Palmer House ballroom. Many, many local Olympians, television personalities and humanitarians were lifted. After the ceremony, we had a private function with the Master. Guru asked if anyone had anything inspiring to say.

A Black woman whom I did not recognize went up to the microphone. I think she was wearing a denim outfit and had her hair in a bun. She addressed Guru as "Gurudev" and mentioned she had been a student of the Master in the early seventies. She said that she had just been released from incarceration for something she had done wrong, and that she was actually in prison when the dreadful events of 11 September occurred. She turned to Guru and said that she couldn't believe those towers no longer existed. As she was speaking, tears were streaming down her face.

Guru said her name with utmost love and then said very soulfully and very seriously, "Your heart's streaming tears and the smiles of my soul shall play hide and seek forever."

MAHIRUHA KLEIN

THE BRAHMIN AND THE DEVOTEE

I like the scene from Guru's play on Lord Krishna, the "Singer of the Eternal Beyond" where a great scholar sees a brahmin holding a copy of the Bhagavad Gita and weeping. He asks the brahmin what part of the Gita he finds difficult to grasp, and offers to explain it to him. The brahmin responds very politely that he understands the Gita perfectly well. He is weeping because whenever he reads this sacred scripture he sees Krishna in his chariot. "These are my psychic tears," he says. The scholar is humbled, and realises that no amount of mental erudition can ever equal genuine spiritual experience.

That's a hard lesson for me to learn because I was raised in the Western tradition which prizes intellectual achievement above all else. Therefore, I always found Guru's spontaneous simplicity so charming and refreshing!

I have started keeping a journal of my experiences with the Master. I have divided it into different themes, like Guru's smiles, Guru's stories, Joy Days with the Master, etc. It has helped me a lot, and I wholeheartedly recommend it as a way of staying inspired and happy.

PRASAD AND HEALTH

I remember that Sri Chinmoy often encourages his students to keep healthy and trim. Once, after a sublime Wednesday night meditation, he inquired of one of his disciples, "I am not insisting, I am not interrogating, I am just asking if you are planning to lose some weight."

The disciple answered, with a little smile in his voice, "I'll be starting a new program soon, Guru."

Then Guru said, "We're in the same boat. I lose weight and then I gain it back."

I think Sri Chinmoy once remarked that realizing God is easier than losing weight!

Anyway, I often found it ironic that Sri Chinmoy would advise us to watch our weight, to stay thin and healthy, often while handing out monster-sized prasad bags of chocolate chip cookies, peanut butter m and m's, Indian Rajbhog butter cookies, eggplant knishes, samosas, ladhus, slices of mushroom pizza and chocolate pudding. And I am not exaggerating! Really! All in one bag!

Devotion of course demanded (and still demands) that I eat everything at one sitting. However, I've come to learn to divide the prasad meal into sweet and savory items and to eat them at different times so I don't get a stomach ache. Usually I eat the savory stuff before going to sleep and the decadent sweets the next morning.

I think he liked watching us eating the prasad. He wasn't that big of an advocate of so-called health foods, often remarking that food has to give joy in order to impart good health. I think he said that bread, rice and potatoes are the best foods to eat to get strength. I don't think `salad' was too high on his list of favorite foods!

Of course, I am not trying to dispense dietary advice here. By all means, follow whatever eating regimen works for you. I'm going over to the local chocolaterie for my daily health infusion. If I pass out from sugar shock, only cinnamon-vanilla crepes will be able to revive me.

See you at the fitness club!

RECOLLECTIONS ON SRI CHINMOY

THE PUBLIC MEDITATIONS

I remember just after I became a student of Sri Chinmoy's in 1997, I used to commute up to Queens once or even twice a week from my college in Trenton. Somehow, the very journey was special. I would drive to the train station in Trenton and then take New Jersey Transit to Penn Station, and then the E and F trains to Queens. As I was a brand new seeker, I would read the Master's books the whole time and commit poems to memory. (My Flute, by Sri Chinmoy, is an absolutely wonderful poetry collection for a new seeker.) Often I would journey on Friday evenings for the seeker meditations.

Oh, God! The seeker meditations were super-cosmic. Sri Chinmoy would come in wearing a beautiful dhoti. He used to wear solid pastel colors like purple or violet or navy blue or pink or white. His entire body radiated a purity and a holiness that I cannot put into words. Just one thing bothered me. I used to experience excruciating head and neck pain at the public meditations. I could not account for it, so I asked my Centre leader for an explanation. He referred me to the following two passages from "The Mind and the Heart in Meditation":

Question: I find public meditations very hard for me. I come in feeling beautiful. Then I feel all this pain coming into my heart and into my head. Am I being attacked? What do you suggest?

Sri Chinmoy: "It is not others' impurity or any other negative force that is entering into you. No. Your difficulty is that when you sit in front, you try to pull far beyond your capacity. When I am on stage, the whole stage is flooded with light. When you sit in front of me and look at me, you try to pull. It is as if you are in a shop and you see all sorts of most beautiful things. Like a greedy fellow you want to buy everything, yet you have in your pocket only five cents. When you try to pull beyond the capacity of your receptivity, at that time you get head pain."

Question: I have no problem in Centre meditations.

Sri Chinmoy: "At the Centre I am not bringing down that kind of light. In a public meditation, the whole hall is flooded with my power, with my light. Right now, I am absolutely normal. But when I am in a public meditation, I am a totally different person. There my consciousness is on a very, very high level. At that time if you try to pull beyond your receptivity, then you are in trouble. It is not that others have been bringing negative forces into you. No! So the best thing for you to do is sit at the back. There the power is less, but if you sit in the front row, you suffer because your capacity is very limited. As you increase your capacity, it will become easy for you to receive more. That is why I always say, 'Don't pull, don't push.'"[4]

Often I would meditate outside the room, in the hallway. The intensity of Light and Peace that he brought down those evenings is something nobody will ever be able to express.

Sometimes, before the meditation, I would grab a quick dinner at Annam Brahma, a vegetarian restaurant in Queens dedicated to the Master's mission. Once I noticed an elderly Black man looking at the television screen, which featured Sri Chinmoy's activities, with utmost devotion. I asked him if he was a student of Sri Chinmoy's. He said no, that he was actually a devotee of Sri Ramakrishna. Then he said, "But Sri Chinmoy is the same thing." He then told me that he had a copy of Guru's book on Ramakrishna's life, "Drink, Drink My Mother's Nectar."

I was touched that a follower of Ramakrishna would rank my Guru in the same class. Of course, both of them showed the unity of all religions in their all-encompassing service and broad humanity.

[4] Sri Chinmoy, *The mind and the heart in meditation*, *Agni Press*, 1977.

MAHIRUHA KLEIN

BEING ALONE WITH THE MASTER

I was alone with Guru only once.

I was guarding the court in May 2003. Pulak pulled up in the driveway in his Toyota (I think that's what it was!) and Guru got out by himself. I opened the gate wide from the inside and held it for Guru. He did not look at me, but as he was walking past he raised his right hand in salutation. I noticed that his hand gesture corresponded exactly with the ancient *abhaya mudra* - the dispeller or destroyer of fear. Many Indian gods and goddesses as well as the Lord Buddha are depicted showing this mudra. As he walked past me, I saw a little smile play on his face. His features radiated the purest calm, serenity and satisfaction I have ever seen. He walked to the back of the driveway, near the Temple. Soon, twelve or thirteen members of Paree's singing group arrived and joined him by the small pond. He taught them a soulful song and then he gave them Prasad. I was standing forty feet away, by the gate, but I heard them singing. Then Guru kindly dismissed them and exited the driveway alone, carrying a single bag of Prasad. As he passed by me, without ever looking at me, he pushed the bag into my arms and kept walking. I thanked him with a surprised and smiling "Thank you, Guru."

I am really grateful for that precious moment with the Master. In my heart, in my soulful imagination, I know there is no limit to the amount of affection and love I can receive from him.

MEMORIES OF DISCIPLES
WHO HAVE PASSED ON

When I came to the Centre in the late 90's, I got to know an old woman from one of the New Jersey Centres. I will call her Alice. Alice had been with Guru about ten years. I think the story of how she came to Guru is interesting.

For many years Alice had been in a terrifying, abusive marriage. Her husband used to find fault with every little thing she did. The only way she could make him stop attacking her was by falling to her knees and crying, asking for his forgiveness. This went on for years and years.

One day, Alice got sick and decided to see a homeopathic doctor in Princeton. This doctor kept some flyers in his office advertising meditation classes. The classes I think were Christian-Science based. She attended these classes and learned a special technique for dealing with angry people: simply sit quietly and count to a hundred out loud.

A week later, while she was eating dinner with her husband, he began criticizing her food and her housekeeping and started screaming. She simply turned around in her chair to face the wall, and slowly began counting to a hundred. She did not apologize. She did not cry.

Her husband had never encountered this before and started saying, "Oh my God, o my God!" as if something was seriously wrong now that she was not caving in and crying!

He went upstairs and went to sleep, not knowing how to deal with it.

He screamed at her a few more times after that, but she simply ignored him, counting to a hundred while facing the wall.

About a month later she visited the homeopath again in Princeton. This time she saw a flyer announcing an upcoming Peace Concert with Sri Chinmoy at Princeton University. She went to the concert and was absolutely stunned by Sri Chinmoy's presence of peace. She told me she had never felt that kind of peace before. To her, Sri Chinmoy was another Jesus Christ. She applied to become a disciple immediately and was accepted.

She started going up to Queens to meditate with the Master, ignoring her husband's repeated threats and screaming fits.

Then, soon after, she had a dream.

In her dream, she was asleep in her bed, when she heard a loud knocking on the door.

"Let me in!" said a loud voice.

She thought it was her husband so she did not open the door.

"Let me in! Let me in!" repeated the voice, accompanied by louder and louder knocks.

Finally, helpless, with nowhere to go, she opened the door with utmost fear and trepidation.

There she saw Sri Chinmoy standing and smiling at her, holding divorce papers.

She divorced her husband a week later, got a restraining order on him, and also the sole ownership of the house.

She stayed with the Master for many years, until her death, and lived an extremely devoted spiritual life.

MEDITATING WITH SRI CHINMOY

I really miss those days when we used to meet at one of two or three public schools, either PS 86 or PS 117. I mean, there was something special about meditating with this great spiritual Master in an enclosed space. When we meditated with him at Aspiration-Ground I felt that his luminous goodwill and compassion diffused and spread all over the world. When we meditated together in the school auditoriums or cafeterias, it was as if the light and grace stayed in the room. You could feel the power in a much more intimate way. The meditations at those schools had more of a family or an ashram feeling.

I did not go on the Christmas trips. But I did not mind because the Wednesday night meditations at Annam Brahma were so beautiful and so soulful. Even though Guru was not physically there, I really felt his presence, his breath, pervading the restaurant. I really have to give the Annam Brahma staff great credit for transforming their restaurant into a beautiful meditation space every week. I also remember Satyajit's group's absolutely sublime performances with great fondness. I enjoyed the congregational feeling in meditating and singing in a private, intimate and sacred space.

MAHIRUHA KLEIN

SEEKERS' EXPERIENCES WITH GURU

(My friends, this story is one hundred percent *unofficial*- I heard it from a friend who heard it from a friend. As I have heard this story confirmed many times, however, I am taking the liberty of retelling it in my own words.)

In 2002, Sri Chinmoy went to Australia for his annual spiritual retreat with a small group of disciples. While he was in the Gold Coast (I think!), he happened to go to a certain barber shop to get his head shaved. The hair stylist stopped in the middle of the job, put down her razor and shook her head.

"I am seeing a woman. Who is this woman I am seeing?" she asked Guru.

Guru looked at her, puzzled. Then, almost on a whim, he pulled out the picture of Mother Kali that he always carried in his wallet.

"Is this the woman you are seeing?" he asked her.

She looked at the image.

"Yes, yes, yes!" she replied.

That night Guru told his disciples this story and said that this hairstylist has a special connection with Mother Kali.

Can you imagine!

THE MASTER'S SCOLDINGS

In the late autumn of 1998, one of Sri Chinmoy's men's singing groups was performing some of his recently composed songs. The Master was not happy with their performance at all. He scolded them for their lack of concern and dedication, and also threatened to disband the group if they did not improve their standard.

"The leader will have to be strict with them," he said.

Then he turned to the group leader, one of his most longtime and most beloved disciples, and said with a big smile and with utmost affection, "Which is an impossible impossibility!"

Eight years later, at the tent in Aspiration Ground, Sri Chinmoy asked for people to come up who were working on a particular project. I was one of the people who came up. When it was my turn to come to the microphone and tell everyone what I was doing, Guru made a comment that I didn't quite understand. I thought he said that I had been sleeping, but I think I was just misunderstanding his English.

"Guru, I was sleeping?" I asked him.

"No!" he said pointedly.

He continued: "You were not sleeping. You were meditating. My disciples do not sleep. They meditate and work. They work and work. I sleep and sleep."

The thing is, I had gotten up really late that morning, for no good reason, and hadn't really done anything the whole day so I blurted out, "I wish!" It was just a dumb thing to say.

Guru seemed a bit caught off guard, but then he turned to

me and gave me a mischievous smile. Then, he shouted, "From tomorrow, work hard!" Then he gave me another cute smile.

Maybe one of the signs of an enlightened being is that he always sees the good in others. Maybe he knows the bad exists, but he pays all attention to the positive. By emphasizing only the positive, he helps the person to be stronger and more divine.

DREAMS OF GURU

Soon after I joined the Centre, I had an interesting dream. I had only been a disciple for a few months. In my dream, I saw I was sitting in an empty classroom in my college. I somehow knew that Sri Chinmoy was about to walk in, and that he was going to give me my spiritual name. I was so excited, because usually people have to wait five or ten years or even longer to get their names, and I was about to get mine after just eight or nine weeks!

Then, sure enough, Sri Chinmoy walked into the classroom, gave me a little smile, and strode up to the chalkboard. He started writing my name on the board. As he wrote each letter, I said it out loud, with great glee.

The first letter was "W". Then came "A". "I" was the next letter. He finished with the letter "T".

Then he turned around and smiled at me again.

I jumped up with joy and screamed, "My name, my name is Wait! My name is Wait! Yes, yes! Hold on?"

It slowly dawned on me that "Wait" was not my name. It was really just an instruction.

Nine years later I got my spiritual name: Mahiruha. It means "Tree" or the "Aspiration-Tree". It was worth waiting for. Of course, one of the main qualities of a tree is patience. Patience is a virtue. Even though I have my spiritual name, I have to remember every day the need for soulful patience-practice. When the Master gives you advice, even in a dream, that advice can be applicable on many levels.

"What is earth? Earth is Eternity's patience-tree. Earth is infinity's flowing compassion."[5]

[5] Sri Chinmoy "Obedience: A Supreme Virtue"

GURU'S DRIVERS

Soon after I moved to New York in December of 2000, someone asked me if I would like to guard Aspiration-Ground for a day. I happily agreed, as I love the meditative atmosphere of the place. I think it was an unusually balmy Wednesday morning, I was wearing my light blue parka, and I was sitting by the gate reading one of Guru's more recent poetry books (maybe a volume from "Seventy-Seven Thousand Service-Trees").

Anyway, at around nine o'clock, Vinaya's car pulls up to the gate and he honks the horn. I noticed there was an elderly Indian man sitting in the passenger seat beside him, whom I took for Prahlad. Vinaya's a good friend of mine, so I opened the gate with an exaggerated bow and a colorful flourish. Then as the car pulled in, "Prahlad" reached out and blessed me a few times with a gentle wave of his hand.

I turned white when I realized it was actually Guru! I mean, Vinaya drives this beaten up Chevrolet station wagon with a faded paint job. I couldn't imagine Guru would want to be driven around in that! I really didn't know that Vinaya was one of Guru's main drivers.

The fact that Guru would be happy with such unassuming portage really impressed me. He always gave us the message of simplicity and humility, and he definitely practiced those virtues in his life.

CUSTOMERS AT ONENESS-FOUNTAIN-HEART

I think I could write thirty books culled from my friends and customers at The Oneness-Fountain-Heart!

One story sticks out in my mind. One Sunday, a meditation group from Rhode Island drove down just to enjoy our Sunday brunch. The leader of the group was just a teenager! Some of the members were in their fifties and sixties. I don't know how she got so many people to meditate with her every week.

Anyway, after they had finished their meal, one of the middle-aged customers beckoned me over. He took out his wallet and he fished out a photograph of himself standing next to Sri Chinmoy by a track in the early eighties. He explained that he had run in a particular half marathon sponsored by the Centre, and afterwards had asked if he might have his picture taken with the Master. Guru agreed.

Guru was so skinny! And he was wearing a bright, red, white and blue track suit. He was smiling from ear to ear, giving a most beautiful and powerful smile.

The man told me that the picture had been taken around 1982, and that he has treasured it ever since.

RECOLLECTIONS ON SRI CHINMOY PART 1

TWO STORIES FROM PRADHAN

I am telling these stories in my own words. Pradhan has told these interesting stories a couple of times in the Chicago Centre, and gave me kind permission to share them in this forum. Any mistakes or inaccuracies are of course completely my own!

In July of 2003 or 2004, Pradhan came to New York to serve as Guru's masseur. Pradhan, as many of you know, is a restauranteur who moonlights as a graphic designer and also, relevant to this story, a chiropractor. He informed Guru of his arrival (his flight arrived sometime in the afternoon) and Guru called him that evening, asking him to come to his house. As soon as Guru saw Pradhan, he said, "Oy, I have been sending you inner messages all this past week, asking you to come! Where have you been?"

Pradhan paused for a moment, and then said. "Guru, just call me. Don't try this inner message business with me! Just call me!"

In 1980, Pradhan experienced a serious crisis in his spiritual life. Guru asked him to come to New York, and gave him a loving but very serious lecture. He finished his talk by telling Pradhan, "Believe me! If you do what I tell you, you will see me everywhere."

Soon after that, when Pradhan was back in Chicago, he was treating a patient at his chiropractic clinic, when he saw Guru in a corner of the room wearing a yellow dhoti. Guru's face had the expression, "I told you so."

While driving home from the clinic, he saw Guru in the rearview mirror, sitting in the back seat wearing a yellow dhoti. Guru was looking at him pointedly, with that same "I told you so" expression.

Perhaps two weeks later, Guru invited Pradhan to return to New York, and to see him at his house. When Pradhan arrived at Guru's porch, he announced his arrival. Shortly thereafter, Guru came out. He sat on the couch across from Pradhan and looked at him for a long time.

Finally, Guru said, "See, I told you so."

MORE MEMORIES FROM ONENESS-FOUNTAIN-HEART

I remember Guru would drop by The Oneness-Fountain-Heart from time to time during the many years that I worked there.

Once he came in by himself, unaccompanied by any of his attendants. I suppose he walked the two miles from his house to the restaurant. I think he was wearing dark blue shorts and a polo shirt. He came quite unexpectedly, in the early afternoon. He entered by the front door and walked quickly through the dining room and then into the kitchen. He did not look at either of us waiters or at anybody else. He seemed very intent on something.

The customers were so electrified! They just looked and looked at Guru in utter amazement.

I walked into the kitchen and did not see Guru. The cook came up to me and whispered that Guru was around the corner, in the dishwashing area. Then Guru emerged from the dishwasher nook. All of us workers by this time were standing by the line (the cooking area), with folded hands. He smiled at us and then left the way he came.

We were all speechless. I asked the cook, "What was Guru doing here?"

"He said, `I am looking for cleanliness.'"

We all looked at each other. Somebody grabbed a broom. Another boy grabbed a small bucket and a couple of rags. Of course I had to go back to taking care of the customers. But we all stayed an extra hour after work that day doing detail cleaning. I think a few weeks after that Guru did stop by to eat with an ambassador-friend. He announced later at one of our regular Wednesday night meditations that our restaurant was very clean.

Thank God!

DRIVING TO SEE THE MASTER

This experience happened perhaps in 2003 or 2004. I remember Guru was talking about his recent concert tour in central Europe. He had given a concert in a certain country. Afterwards, there was a function just for disciples. Guru mentioned some ex-disciples had driven practically across Europe to see the Master, and they had approached one of his attendants, asking if they could possibly sit in on the function. Guru said that he had personally asked these people to leave the Centre; they did not choose to leave. The guard did not want to admit them, but they asked repeatedly and soulfully, so he finally approached Guru with their request. Guru said that since they had driven so many hours unconditionally that they should be allowed to just take prasad. He said they passed by him as they took the prasad, and he smiled at them.

Guru was touched by their devotion and love.

MIRACLES

Many years ago, before I became a disciple, I used to go swimming at my college pool. Sometimes I would see an old woman there who would do stretching exercises at the shallow end of the pool and from time to time we would have discussions.

She confided in me that she had been diagnosed with terminal brain cancer in the early nineties; the doctors had given up all hope. Soon after that, she saw a flyer for a meditation workshop given by students of Sri Chinmoy. As she was depressed and despondent she decided that she may as well use her remaining time wisely, so she went to the seminar to learn to meditate.

She told me that as she looked at Sri Chinmoy's Transcendental photograph, that tears of joy welled up and streamed down her face; she felt absolutely bathed in divine love and light and reassurance. Two weeks after she attended the class, she went for a routine check up. The doctors returned with the test results looking baffled. They told her that her tumor had stopped growing, completely. It had not disappeared, but it was no longer malignant. They simply could not understand it. They told her that they felt she would be fine. That was many years ago, and last time I spoke with her, she confirmed that the cancer has never returned.

She told me that since that time she meditates for half an hour every morning and offers her deepest gratitude to the Power that so kindly granted her a life-extension.

SEPTEMBER 11

It's hard to believe eleven years have passed since September 11, 2001. I recall I was working at The Oneness-Fountain-Heart that morning, stocking the waiters' refrigerator with cokes and sprites, when the cook rushed in and told me that a plane had struck the World Trade Center. We kept our restaurant open the whole day. The restaurant, with its calming blue colors, beautiful fountains, and videos of Guru meditating or playing instruments was like an oasis, not only us, but also for the customers.

The thing I most remember from that day and the few weeks that followed, was the incredible sweetness of the New York people. Such heart! Such courage! I'll never forget the feeling of family and oneness that spread over the city and lasted for a long time.

During the first three or four days after September 11, however, I was in a state of total shock. I couldn't meditate, I could just think of the unthinkable tragedy and loss.

The Saturday following the disaster, we had our regular Saturday night meeting at Aspiration-Ground. Guru offered a most soulful and beautiful message in tribute to the victims and also in honor of the self-giving soul of America.

"At this juncture our only bounden Duty is to identify our prayerful hearts with the innocent, harmless and helpless victims and their beloved ones.

Our tearful eyes and the bleeding hearts of the relatives and friends have already touched the Compassion-Feet of our Absolute Lord Beloved Supreme. He is with His Infinity's Compassion-Affection-Love Sweetness-Fondness taking care of His supremely chosen children who have recently arrived at His Heaven-Home.

May America the Beautiful forever shine bright-brighter-brightest in the Heart of God the Creator and God the Creation."

– Sri Chinmoy, September 2001

He also offered his deepest gratitude to the Supreme that everybody in our spiritual family was ok. He had Paree's group come up and sing "Rakhe Krishna Mare Ke, Mare Krishna Rakhe Ke", an ancient Indian saying which he had set to music. It has to do with trusting God and leaving ourselves in His care. It is a most haunting and comforting song.

At the end of the meditation, we had a walk-past. I had been unable to absorb Guru's reassuring words because I was still so shaken. But as I passed by him, Guru leaned forward and said into the microphone, "Remain happy. If you can stay happy, then the forces will not be able to do anything. Remain happy."

I don't want Sri Chinmoy's words to be misinterpreted here.

He was absolutely not saying that we should be happy over that catastrophe! He was just saying that we have to bring our spirituality forward when terrible things happen. We do this through our inner happiness, which implies praying, meditating and trying to inspire the people around us.

Through maintaining our spiritual happiness, we keep ourselves centered. When he talks about "forces" he's referring to the wild, ignorant forces that want to keep us in a state of panic and anguish. We can make big mistakes when we lose our inner balance. It just becomes a spiral. Poise, calmness and dignity are the best ways to meet tragedy and disaster, no matter the scale. And that's one of the most valuable life lessons I ever learned from my Master.

"The inner worlds
And the outer world
Are clashing and crashing together.
Yet my Beloved Lord Supreme
Has kept me
Absolutely unshaken." [6]

[6] Sri Chinmoy, "My Christmas-New Year-Vacation-Aspiration-Prayers" (Part 14)

MAHIRUHA KLEIN

CHANCE ENCOUNTERS

Sometime around 2004 (pardon the vagueness!) Guru met with former Soviet President Mikhail Gorbachev. They met at a hotel in Manhattan. Before President Gorbachev arrived, Guru was sitting with his interpreter in the lobby. The woman sitting next to Guru apologized because her cell phone was going off. She took the call, and then informed Guru excitedly that her sister had just given birth to fraternal twins, a boy and a girl. Incidentally, she had never met Guru before, and did not know he was a spiritual Master. Guru just said, "I am blessing them."

A RECOLLECTION ON GURU'S HOMEOPATHIST FRIEND, DR. CHER

When I moved to New York in 2000, I met a kind, self-effacing Chinese doctor named Dr. Cher. He told me that his name was not actually Dr. Cher, but that Americans were manifestly incapable of pronouncing his actual name, so Dr. Cher would have to do.

He was a very simple man with a big smile and a big heart. He lived close to Annam Brahma and would often treat disciples for little or no money. He was an herbalist.

Disciples always told me that they didn't find his remedies very effective. But nobody else was better at taking away Guru's pain! For us, maybe he wasn't such a great doctor. But he was special to Guru.

One night, when Guru and most of the disciples were away during our annual Christmas Trip holiday, I was surprised to see Dr. Cher at our Annam Brahma meditation. He told me he had become a disciple. He would keep his hands folded during virtually the entire meeting.

Alas, a few months later he himself got very sick and had to go to the hospital. By that time Guru had returned from abroad. Guru was very concerned for Dr. Cher and sent Databir and other disciples to the intensive care ward to look after him around the clock. In spite of their best efforts and Guru's good will, Dr. Cher died. Guru actually came to the hospital before Dr. Cher passed. I think he was in the room with Dr. Cher. He begged the doctors not to give up, to do just one more thing to help his beloved Chinese doctor, but they wouldn't do it. Guru said later that they could have saved Dr. Cher. He said ruefully that in India doctors listen to him, but in America they don't listen. I have rarely ever seen Guru so upset.

He said that he had asked the doctors to give him a certain treatment, which is just standard procedure for the condition that Dr. Cher had. But the doctors wouldn't do it.

Guru said that the morning after Dr. Cher died, that he asked Vinaya to drive him all the way up Main Street to Bayside, so that he could do his morning walk and exercises. He said that he saw so many Chinese people. He said that he saw two old Chinese men walking together, only one was walking in the regular manner, while the other one was walking backwards. They were talking, he commented, in their "pok-pok" language and laughing.

An old Chinese woman saw Guru walking so pitifully and said to him, "You are not well, you are not well."

Guru said to her that she was right, that he was not feeling well at all. The woman was carrying a stick, maybe a walking stick, and she held it up and pointed it at Guru and said, "I am giving you energy! I give you energy!"

Guru said that the woman was trying to help him, but that he felt much worse after she gave him that energy infusion.

He commented that it was Dr. Cher's soul that was bringing so many Chinese people to him, that was showing him the sweetness of the Chinese people.

Then Guru recited a poem he wrote for Dr. Cher. He said that, like us, he could not pronounce his real name properly. But he preferred to call him Dr. Choo.

The poem goes something like this. (It is from memory and totally unofficial)

Dr. Choo, Dr. Choo, Dr. Choo Who are you? Who are you? Who are you?

"I was your friend I became your admirer I became your adorer I became your disciple I am ignorance-destruction-rifle."

Guru was so grateful to his friends like Dr. Cher who helped him and who helped his spiritual children. Guru never forgot the people who loved him and helped him.

MAHIRUHA KLEIN

GURU'S INTERVIEWS

Once in the early eighties, Sri Chinmoy was being interviewed by a well-known radio host who specialized in the occult and paranormal phenomena. He happened to ask Sri Chinmoy a sincere spiritual question, which the Master answered. But the answer left the radio announcer completely flabbergasted. He had never heard someone speak about spiritual matters with such fluency and authority. He couldn't talk, and Sri Chinmoy didn't say anything either. This silence lasted for about thirty seconds. Then the host said to himself, "Oh no! On radio, if you don't say anything, nothing happens!" So he asked Guru some more questions and they had a nice conversation.

I had the chance to meet this radio and television personality once. He is a very intelligent and a very sincere and gracious individual.

QUESTIONS AND ANSWERS

Six years ago, I asked Sri Chinmoy about his own feelings or perceptions about Bach and Beethoven. He began his response by wondering if there was anyone in the world who knew less about them than he did. He paused for just a few seconds, and then began to speak quietly, but somehow with real authority. He spoke about them for ten minutes, offering what he called his "inner observations" on their lives and music. He told me that he did have occasion in his life to listen to their music. Still, I was shocked by the depth of detail in his analysis of their musical styles.

How did Sri Chinmoy answer the question so well? I do not think Sri Chinmoy was very well read in the field of classical music. I am just saying this because in my ten years of studying with him personally, I never heard him bring up the subject even once. I think he was using his third eye to answer the question; he used his inner vision.

I might even go so far as to say that he may not have even been using any occult power to answer this question. I am just speculating here.

I am sure many of you are familiar with this aphorism from Twenty-Seven Thousand Aspiration-Plants:

"In spiritual communication,
Mental telepathy

Is the beginners' course." [7]

I asked an elderly disciple what this means, because I had always thought mental telepathy to be a very high attainment. He clarified the aphorism for me, saying that mental telepathy is just the first step in using the heart. In other words, if someone is extremely spiritually developed, then he or she doesn't need to read my mind to know everything about me. Through completely identifying with me, through immediate oneness, my experience and my life immediately become his life. There is no need to consciously *do* anything or to apply any kind of occult or spiritual power. In complete oneness, total and exhaustive knowledge is already there.

In response to a question by one of his guards about overcoming weaknesses, Sri Chinmoy responded that the most effective way to remove the hurdles in our life is through love of God. I'd like just to excerpt a couple sentences from his answer, which can be found in the twenty-third volume of "Sri Chinmoy Answers".

> "This whole world is run by a Power. We call it the Cosmic Knowledge, the Cosmic Wisdom, the Cosmic Power. Where has that Power come from? It has come from God's Love. God's Love created the Cosmic Power, and we can enter into the Cosmic Power when we love God."

I like that idea that God's Love is precedential to God's

[7] Sri Chinmoy, *Twenty-Seven Thousand Aspiration-Plants*, part 269, Agni Press, 1998

Power. I think that's why Sri Chinmoy was able to answer the question so quickly. He just used his universal oneness-heart and became inseparably one with the consciousness and life of Bach and of Beethoven. From that position of absolute identification and oneness, he was able to speak so clearly, so confidently and so thoroughly. And that suggests a power that far surpasses any occult or psychic attainment.

Just my opinion!

GURU ON HEALING

I remember once, maybe in 2006, when Guru spoke about an elderly Englishwoman he had met a long time ago. I think Sushumna took Guru to see her. She was a healer, but, unfortunately, she was suffering from many, many terrible diseases. Guru commented to us that this particular woman did have the capacity to take diseases from people. But she did not have the ability to dispose of those diseases. She could only take them into her own body. He seemed so sorry for her.

I remember a husband and wife who used to come to the weekly Friday seeker meetings. The wife was extremely ill, and needed her husband's assistance to get on and off the stage. I don't think they came to the meditation for the wife to be cured, necessarily. They just recognized that Sri Chinmoy was a real spiritual Master and they wanted to participate in his soulful programs. They came for many years.

I really appreciate the sincere seekers like them who came to pray and meditate with the Master. I really got a lot of inspiration from their soulful devotion to Guru and their own intense inner cry. Guru said once that some people make very fast spiritual progress just from reading his writings. They may never see Sri Chinmoy physically, but by reading his spiritual writings devotedly they can make real progress.

I think Sri Chinmoy tried to avoid public demonstrations of his spiritual healing capacities. I believe he preferred to work in secret, because it was more effective and also so that people would not come to him just so that he would resolve their ailments.

Sri Chinmoy did cure me of a terrible respiratory condition. I've mentioned this before. I had not even met him, but had started meditating on a picture of the Master in a high consciousness and had also started reading his books. To this day, I am grateful to be able to breathe normally.

How much I take for granted!

MAHIRUHA KLEIN

A MEMORY FROM THE ONENESS-FOUNTAIN-HEART RESTAURANT

I think in early 2005, Sri Chinmoy met with an ambassador friend of his at The Oneness-Fountain-Heart Restaurant. We (the waitstaff and the whole restaurant) were given ample notice, so we were very happy to be fully prepared to welcome Sri Chinmoy and his friend. I think Guru did most of the talking. He spoke very quickly and passionately about Indian history, his own experiences in America and the world situation. The Ambassador listened very attentively.

The ambassador had to leave after an hour, so Sri Chinmoy stayed and had some tea and a chocolate mousse dessert. Then he got up to leave. Maybe ten feet from the door, he paused, and looked around the restaurant.

"Beautiful, beautiful," he said.

Then he turned to us, the workers, and said, "To me this is not a restaurant. It is like a beautiful Indian temple. Here I feel sweetness and purity. In life, if you have sweetness and purity, what else do you need?"

Then Guru smiled at us and left.

COOKING IS IN THE HAND

I remember a talented chef at The Oneness-Fountain-Heart Restaurant mentioned casually to one of Guru's attendants that he'd like to create a cookbook. When the attendant mentioned this idea to Guru, Guru said, "Cooking is not in a book. Cooking is in the hand."

I like the fact that Guru could speak with perfect confidence and authority about any subject. In one of the Sri Chinmoy Answers books he gives a famous marathon runner very specific, concrete advice about running.

Cooking is in the hand. I suppose that means that to learn how to be a great cook, you have to watch the hands of a cook, see what he does, how his fingers touch and interact with the food.

How grateful I am to have a spiritual teacher who can answer any question!

MEDITATION CONTESTS

During the Christmas Trips, Guru often held meditation contests. He would give a special Prasad, often a piece of fruit, to whoever did the best meditation. One of my friends served as Guru's attendant for many years. Guru sometimes asked him to serve as a monitor during some of these special meditation contests. I think people would sometimes walk up to Guru in a line, meditate in front of him, sit down again, and then the next group of people would come up to meditate. I actually don't know how these "contests" operated, as I never attended a Christmas Trip. But, anyway, Guru gave my friend special instructions about how many people should come up at a time, how they should be seated, etc. But he had trouble understanding Guru, and wasn't exactly sure what Guru wanted. It seemed a little complicated.

At one point, Guru got frustrated or upset with the way my friend was handling the flow of people. So, my friend the guard prayed in silence, saying, "Guru, you are also my inner Guru. So, I am praying to you, as my inner Guru, to help me deal with the outer Guru."

Then Guru gave my friend the fruit Prasad (or in this case, a carton of soymilk!) for having done the best meditation! He had gone deep within and approached the Universal Guru within the outer Guru. Maybe that's all that Guru really wanted from my friend in the first place!

PEACE BLOSSOM COLLEGES

In 1999 and 2000, one young woman in our New York Centre began dedicating colleges and universities as Sri Chinmoy Peace Blossoms. She would get in touch with the Presidents or members of the Board and ask them if they would like to participate in this program for world harmony and friendship. Many, many colleges responded affirmatively, often with great enthusiasm.

After a sublime Friday night public meditation at Aspiration Ground, after the seekers had left, she approached the microphone to give news about her latest success. Sri Chinmoy interrupted her before she could even say anything!

"Why, why, why does your smile not have its usual luminosity and brilliance and power?" he groaned.

He continued, saying, "If you are suffering physically, I sympathize with you. If you are suffering mentally, I am sorry."

"Guru, I'm tired!" She answered.

Guru didn't miss a beat.

"Are you the only one who works?" he asked her. "Are the rest of us all vagabonds?"

"Whatever," she said, taking Guru's teasing in stride.

She went on to describe her latest successful effort. She said that she had just been on the phone with the president of a particular college, and she mentioned Guru's name. The president was surprised to hear the name "Sri Chinmoy" because his roommate in college had been a disciple! The president had actually roomed with this young man before he had become Guru's student. He mentioned that Guru clearly had a positive impact on his friend's life. He still remembered that. He was happy to dedicate the college as a Sri Chinmoy Peace Blossom.

The young woman said she didn't ask what the president's roommate's name was. We would like to have known.

She then smiled and told Guru that this was something like the fortieth Peace Blossom College. Everyone cheered and clapped. Guru seemed very pleased.

GURU'S MEMORIES OF SRI AUROBINDO

Sri Chinmoy had absolutely the deepest, lifelong love, adoration and admiration for his beloved Guru, Sri Aurobindo. He gave almost eight hundred Peace Concerts around the world, and at every single one he would sing songs in honour of his great mentor and spiritual giant, Sri Aurobindo. I remember two things that Guru said about his discipleship with the Master.

He said that he never had occasion to speak a single word to his Master. In other words, his relationship with his Guru was completely on the inner plane. Some of Sri Aurobindo's disciples served their Master personally, round the clock, as his secretaries or stenographers or editors (like Sri Chinmoy, Sri Aurobindo was very involved in literary work). For years, Guru washed the dishes at the Ashram hall. That was his job and he liked it because it was a simple job. It gave him much time to meditate and read. I guess this goes to show that it is not the outer relationship that is most important, but rather the disciple's receptivity and openness to the Master's light. I think I remember Guru saying that his best disciples were three people in Russia that he had yet to meet, but who meditated on him with utmost devotion. I like this passage from "Sri Chinmoy Answers" part 9:

"There is one disciple whose name I do not want to say, but she is an elderly lady. O God! She says that wherever I go, or wherever she moves, from this room to that room and another room, always she sees me, she feels me. Now, where is her city, and where is New York? She is not in New York. Perhaps I will never in this lifetime see that person on the physical plane. Never, never! But it is not her mental hallucination. Only on the strength of imagination, everywhere she sees me right in front of her, beside her, everywhere."

Guru also spoke about his final *darshan* with the Master. All of the disciples, including Guru, would pass before the Master four times year. Each disciple was allowed to stand in front of the Master for four seconds, not more. I think Guru's job was to take everybody's shoes from the entrance of the hall and put them by the exit, just so that people would not have to go back to get their shoes. Because of this duty, he was often one of the last people to pass by the Master. At Sri Aurobindo's last darshan, perhaps in 1949 or 1950, Guru was the one of the last, if not the very last person to receive blessing of the Master's silent gaze. When he stood in front of the Master, he saw that tears were streaming down Sri Aurobindo's face. Guru told us that Sri Aurobindo was shedding tears because it was the last time they would see each other on the physical plane. He knew that he was going to leave the body soon.

I like this story.

GURU'S MEMORIES FROM SRI AUROBINDO ASHRAM

These are just a couple more of Sri Chinmoy's recollections from his days in the Sri Aurobindo ashram.

Once Guru mentioned that nobody in the Aurobindo ashram would look at anybody else directly in the eye. Guru explained the spiritual significance behind this practice, saying that when you look at somebody in the eye, you can receive something from that person; you can give something to that other person; you can lose something of your own.

Guru also expressed sadness that so few of his disciples would bring his books to read before our Wednesday night meditation. He said many years ago that he would like all of his students to read his books for at least half an hour a day. I think he may have even commented that if we don't have the time to read his books, that we should just look at them. Look at the covers at least! When he lived at the Sri Aurobindo ashram, Guru explained, he read all of Sri Aurobindo's books at least eight times. Considering Sri Aurobindo's voluminous output, that is quite a remarkable statement!

We've formed a poetry club here at the Chicago Centre. We read out Guru's poems and we try to discuss what his poems mean to us. Here's a topical poem:

MAHIRUHA KLEIN

WHO WILL READ MY POEMS?

"Who will read my poems?
Man? Never!
Since he has so many
Important things to do,
I just forgive him.

"Who will read my poems?
God? Why not?
He has to,
Since it is He who
Has written all these poems
In and through me.

"Naturally He has to
And
He always does,
Carefully,
Lovingly,
Cheerfully." [8]

[8] Sri Chinmoy, *The Wings of Light*, part 14, Agni Press, 1974.

GURU AT YORK COLLEGE

Sometimes York College would hold special functions for international events. In 2005, York College hosted the international Ramayana conference, which drew thousands of devout Hindus from all over the world. They asked Sri Chinmoy to open the weeklong program with a spiritual meditation. I just remember Guru playing the esraj, and singing a lively song, with the words, "Sri Ramachandra, Sri!" He smiled to himself while singing, he seemed happy. He may have also sung "Sri Ramachandra, Adi Avatar". I believe Adi Avatar means "first Avatar" or, perhaps figuratively, "Avatar pioneer". The conference organizer, when he introduced Guru, said, "I would like to welcome Sri Chinmoy, the great Yogi. If any Indian has accomplished something for the world, he has." His words about Guru were so heartfelt.

The following year, the local Bangladeshi community convened a symposium on Bangladeshi youth, with the theme, "Next generation not to be lost." They also invited Sri Chinmoy the open the program. The conference organizer invited Sri Chinmoy to stand him with on stage, and he welcomed Guru with folded hands. The Master took his hands in his own and meditated with the gentleman for perhaps five seconds, and then bowed his head to him. Then Sri Chinmoy sat down on a simple folding chair on the stage and began reading out some of his own English poetry on the theme of childhood, simplicity and innocence. I just remember the room was filled with crying and screaming Bengali children and their mothers, and that Guru seemed to radiate a childlike consciousness I had not seen for a long time. When he finished reading his poems, he walked back and forth on the stage, walking somehow like a child, almost stomping. Because he was surrounded by so many children, he became a child, too.

After Guru had finished and left the stage, some traditional Bengali dancers, all young women, went up. They danced to a song that had something to do with Krishna. In the course of the performance, whenever Krishna's name was mentioned, the dancers would fold their hands high over their heads in a gesture of obeisance. I didn't think they did traditional Hindu dances in Bangladesh anymore, but I guess I was wrong.

Both of these conferences were special opportunities for Guru to offer his unique inspiration to the local Indian community. They were very sweet experiences!

GURU'S MEETINGS WITH OTHER MASTERS

I haven't been posting any recollections recently, and people may feel that I simply don't have any more recollections to share, but that is not the case. It's simply I do not know where to begin.

How is it possible anyway to convey a life as miraculous as Sri Chinmoy's? I mean, he never did anything or said anything that did not have profound meaning. Even his cute jokes or casual, funny remarks carried deep truth.

In the early autumn of 2006, Guru played for us the taped footage of his visit to the ashram of another spiritual Master, a Sufi Sheikh, who is based in upstate New York. The two Masters agreed that they would hand out prasad to the disciples of the other Master. When the disciples of the other Guru took the prasad from Sri Chinmoy's hands, they genuflected in front of him with utmost sincerity, crossing their arms over their chests in the ancient eastern tradition. Then they took the Prasad from him with absolutely the most devoted, respectful attitude. Some of them were shedding tears.

But when Guru's disciples took the prasad from the other Master, I am sorry to say, they took the fruit in a much more perfunctory, almost nonchalant way. They just filed past him and took the fruit in a casual manner. In defense of my spiritual brothers and sisters, I have to say that Guru almost always told us not to take our time while taking prasad. Sometimes he would even say at the end of a long seven-hour meditation, "Take the prasad and disappear." Still, Guru was a little upset when he saw that and remarked, "Look at the difference between the way the disciples of the other Master take prasad from me and how my disciples take it!"

This Master, and, in fact, his entire family have always been extremely, extremely kind to Guru and to his spiritual children. I don't want to mention his name on a public forum, but I have always admired this Teacher, his lofty writings and true spiritual dynasty.

HOW "DAVID" CAME TO THE CENTRE

In early July of 1976, disciples from St. Louis, Kansas City, Milwaukee and Chicago met in a farm house in St. Louis for a joy weekend. Those terms, "joy day" and "joy weekend" did not exist back then, but the concept was there. They knew that Guru was planning on calling them on Sunday morning, at around eleven o'clock. They began meditating at around ten o'clock, most soulfully, and Guru did call them at eleven. One of the disciples had installed a special speaker on the phone so that everybody could hear Guru.

Guru asked how many people were there and they told him, and then Guru asked to speak to each person individually. David did not go up to talk to Guru because he was not yet a disciple and had yet to make up his mind. Finally, after Guru had spoken to and had blessed each disciple who was there personally, he asked, "Hey, is there anybody else?"

The disciples all looked at each other. Finally, one of them approached the phone and said, "Yes Guru, there is one seeker here but he is not a disciple."

Guru indicated that he wanted to talk to this seeker, so David went up to the phone.

"What is your name?" Guru asked.

David told him.

"How long have you been coming to the Centre?" Guru inquired.

"Two months, Guru," David said.

"Oy!" Guru exclaimed, "Two months and still you have not

made up your mind!"

"Guru," David said, "I just did."

Guru laughingly said, "You just did?"

Then Guru fell silent for about ten seconds. Everyone sensed that Guru was meditating. Kalyan, the St. Louis Centre leader, told me he could feel Guru's meditation-power, his vibration, flood the room. "All right," Guru said suddenly.

"I am accepting you," he continued, "Accept our path wholeheartedly as I am accepting you. Try to be a good Chicago Sri Chinmoy Centre member, and always listen to Sandy the Great!" (Pradhan)

Then David sat down, more or less stunned, and Guru concluded his blessingful phone call by giving a poem: "Life is like a lotus – petal by petal the lotus blossoms. At the end of our journey's close we offer this fully blossomed lotus at the Feet of the Supreme" (my recollection of David's words, so not official).

Regarding the portion of his discussion with Guru where he asked him to always listen to Pradhan, David said that he listened to Pradhan for about a day. Pradhan laughed and said that David listened to him for a total of ten minutes!

HOW JYOTIPRIYA GOT HER SPIRITUAL NAME

Many years ago, a woman from one of the European Centres told me an amusing story about how she got her spiritual name from Guru.

This was sometime in the early 1970's. Guru had just given a talk in London and there was an informal function afterwards. This lady had accompanied Guru for his entire European lecture tour, as had her best friend, who was from the same Centre. Suddenly, Guru called her friend up on stage and blessed her. Then he gave her a spiritual name. It was a very beautiful name, with a lengthy, elaborate meaning. It took Guru some five minutes to explain and interpret the full significance of her name. She was visibly overwhelmed!

Then Guru called up this particular woman, who was a Centre leader (her Centre was quite small). He gave her her spiritual name and then supplied the meaning: "She who loves the light and who is beloved by the light."

Guru paused for a second and then said, "That's it."

This woman laughed when she told me this, remarking that it was if Guru was saying, in his own loving way, "And you're lucky you got that!"

MY OWN WORLD

On some Sunday in late March, 2005, I got up late. I meditated a little bit and then decided to go out for a rare run. Then, as now, my runs involve a great deal of walking. Anyway, I was "running" along Union Turnpike, and had just passed the Madal Bal bakery on my right, when I saw a car that looked an awful lot like Pulak's station wagon. There was an Indian man in the front passenger seat.

Guru!

There was a lot of traffic, so the car was going very slowly. I did not attract attention to myself, but just folded my hands as I ran. Guru turned his head to the side and saw me and recognized me. Then he immediately looked away. The logjam cleared up and the car started moving again and soon vanished far ahead of me.

I was so happy that I had seen Guru. True, he did not smile or wave at me, but I knew that Guru often went on long, soulful drives, to nowhere in particular. During these long drives he would just meditate and meditate. And sometimes he would chant "Supreme" hundreds and hundreds of times, softly and prayerfully. I was really happy to have even seen him, just for a moment.

Anyway, the following Sunday was warm and sunny and Guru held a meditative function at Aspiration-Ground. At the end of the function, prasad (maybe vanilla crème wafers and semi-ripe bananas) was placed in crates in front of him and we all formed a line to take it.

Just a couple seconds after I had taken prasad, Guru leaned towards the microphone and said, "Last week I saw Morris running on Union Turnpike. I was calling him, but he was in his own world."

Guru was calling me? He didn't roll down the window as far as I saw. Had he been calling me inside the car, hoping I would read his lips? I did fold my hands and look at him. How was I in my own world? I suppose Guru wanted me to feel special, that he could tell everyone that he had been calling my name but that I was too proud to acknowledge him!

Guru, you can call me anytime, however you want to. Just remember: I do have caller ID.

MAHIRUHA KLEIN

LOVE OFFERINGS

The first week of June in 2004 was rather warm and overcast. On that Friday, I got off my shift at The Oneness-Fountain-Heart at three o'clock. My bike had recently had its seat torn off (welcome to Jamaica ...Queens), so I was walking home. I had got to Union Turnpike when the sky opened up in a full-blown summer storm. It rained with tremendous intensity for about five minutes and then cleared up almost immediately. A beautiful rainbow appeared in the sky, floating over and beyond the wisps of dark clouds. An Afghani woman and her daughter saw it before I did. The mother pointed to it out to her daughter and her daughter looked up and I also looked and saw it. So beautiful.

That night I wrote Guru a letter thanking him for showing me that beautiful rainbow, and that I felt his grace operating in many areas of my life. I included a fifty-dollar bill.

The following evening I arrived late at the Saturday function because I worked the dinner shift. Guru had just called for love-offering (completely voluntary donations from people who are in a position to give). So I ran up on stage and put my letter in the box. Guru nodded as I passed by him. I just got the sense that he was pleased not only with the fact that I was offering money, but also because I was giving with the right attitude, with a sense of joy. I also felt that he knew about my experience without my even telling him. He intuited why I was giving this money and that mattered more to him than the actual gift.

Here's poem 109 from the first volume of "Seventy-Seven Thousand Service-Trees":

"The sun is in the west,
A rainbow is in the east,
But I am neither in the sun
   Nor in the rainbow.
I am only in God's Satisfaction." [9]

[9] Sri Chinmoy, Seventy-Seven Thousand Service-Trees, part 1, Agni Press, 1998

MAHIRUHA KLEIN

MEDITATIONS WITH GURU

During a meditation function in the early months of 1999 (perhaps it was late February), Guru stood up and folded his hands and said, "King Hussein."

Everyone in the room stood up and we all meditated in a few minutes in silence. In all my years with Guru, I never had that experience before or after. It was as if King Hussein's soul came to Guru and Guru wanted to honor him with a collective meditation.

I do not believe Guru was ever able to meet with this great and humane peace maker, but I know that Guru esteemed him very highly. After the two or three minutes of silent meditation, various people read out tributes to King Hussein from world leaders. I believe former US President Bill Clinton was present at King Hussein's funeral and someone remembered his tribute to King Hussein's wife, Noor. He had called her "the daughter of America and the Queen of Jordan."

GURU'S ADVICE TO ME

Shortly after I became a disciple in 1997, I posed a question to Guru, through my Centre leader, as to whether or not I should continue my formal education. I was about to graduate from college, and was just wondering if Guru might have any insights as to the best course of action for me.

She got back to me promptly. She saw Guru at one of our Divine Enterprises and posed the question to him.

"Do you know who Morris is, Guru?" she began.

Guru did not know me by name, so she gave a description and Guru said, "Yes, I see him often." I had been attending both the seeker meditations and the Wednesday night meditations regularly. I was living near Trenton, New Jersey and took the train up biweekly to see the Master.

"Guru," she continued, "Morris was wondering whether or not he should go to graduate school. He is about to graduate from college."

Guru meditated for a moment or two and said, "He does not have to go to school anymore. He should just get a job and it should have a nice atmosphere."

Then Guru smiled at my Centre leader and said, "Today would have been your mother's birthday. I am blessing her soul in heaven."

I get a lot of joy by remembering this communication between my Guru and my Centre leader. It just shows how committed Guru was to being a Guru, to giving each of his students personal attention and guidance. He told me to work as opposed to get more academic training. But he only told me that after he had meditated and received that message from within.

In general, I know that he asks people not to go back to school because he wants his students to focus more on developing themselves spiritually as opposed to intellectually. But he has asked some people to study when he saw that that would be conducive to their spiritual growth.

> "My deep heart is full.
> I shall smile today,
> Heaven's blue smile.
> I shall study once more
> In my inner school
> And scatter God-Light all around,
> For a while." [10]

---

[10] Sri Chinmoy, *A soulful cry versus a fruitful smile*, Agni Press 1977.

MORE ADVICE FROM GURU

I mentioned how in answer to one question, Guru asked me not to study anymore, but to just get a job with a nice atmosphere. I followed Guru's recommendation and worked a variety of retail and marketing jobs until I eventually moved to New York and worked in one of the restaurants associated with the Centre for about seven years. In 2007, I decided to look for a position in a more academic field, perhaps as a librarian or researcher. I felt that more training, or graduate-level study, would probably be necessary to get that kind of position.

Shortly after Guru's birthday in 2007, I attended an open-house, an information session offered by the Queens Public Library about a special work-study program that would lead to a Master's degree in library science. It seemed like a good idea to me. I didn't mention it to Guru because I wanted to attend the seminar and get a good idea about the program first.

As it was the tail end of Celebrations there were still many visitors. So, from the seminar, I went straight home, got ready for the meditation and arrived at Aspiration-Ground just in time to take prasad.

I saw that Guru was in a very good mood, smiling and smiling at all the bright, aspiring visitors who had come to honor his birthday. But, when I passed by him, his smile vanished. I saw his expression turn into one of utmost unhappiness and yes, shocked despair.

I took the prasad and went home. Guru's very evident

discomfort gave me pause. But, honestly, I had not liked the presenter at the open house…at all. Also, for some reason I couldn't put my finger on, the whole program struck me as somehow odd and wrong.

A few nights later, I had an interesting dream. I was by myself at Oneness-Fountain-Heart, the restaurant was empty and dim. The tables had all been cleared to one side of the room. Only a single solitary chair remained in the middle of the dining area. Then, quite unexpectedly, Guru walked in and sat down on the chair. He looked at me and then put his hand over his heart and said softly, "Study the inner library."

I found Guru's words really helpful. Guru always followed Thomas Jefferson's maxim to take things by the smooth handle, or to deal with people in the most polite and gracious way possible. He did not tell me not to get this further education towards a library science degree. He just told me to study the inner library. In other words, whether or not I want to listen to the Master on the outer plane, if I aspire, if I pray and meditate, then I will do the right thing at the right time. To study the inner library means to practise the spiritual life in all its many different aspects, including all the soulful activities to which Guru contributed so much: reading, praying, meditating, running, serving.

Again, Guru's hundreds and hundreds of books also make up the "inner library". By reading his books I can stay in his consciousness and acquire all the education I will ever really need to be spiritual on this earth. In his own gentle way, Guru is telling me that he is not prohibiting me from getting outer degrees, no. He is just saying that if I really aspire and really read his books with devotion, then I will know what to do in my outer life, and will be able to judge whether or not more formal education will accelerate my progress.

I have taken the path of doing simple, menial jobs that free me up to spend a lot of time in prayer and spiritual study. That's the path that works best for me, and I also feel that this is the conclusion that Guru was guiding me towards in his own humble, down-to-earth way.

"The book of your heart's light
Is an excellent book.
Keep it always on your reading desk
To serve as your ever-ready reference book,
Especially when you enter into
The library of ignorance-night."[11]

[11] *Sri Chinmoy, Ten Thousand Flower-Flames, part 76, Agni Press, 1983.*

MAHIRUHA KLEIN

SRI CHINMOY'S 1999 ESRAJ ANNIVERSARY

When Sri Chinmoy came back from the Christmas trip in late January of 1999, I remember he gave a special esraj concert at PS 117, in the small, intimate auditorium. The concert commemorated the anniversary of his esraj playing. I just remember watching him play his favorite melodies, he always held my attention with his superb musicianship. It seemed like a different kind of esraj than the one he played earlier, somehow simpler in design, with a beautiful tone. He wore a gold dhoti, if I remember correctly. As I watched him play, his brow furrowed in concentration, his arm moving in measured arcs, I felt myself enter into a kind of tranced-out bliss. I felt all my problems were melting away into nothingness, all that mattered was this soulful music. I've always loved Sri Chinmoy's esraj music – The Beauty of a Oneness-Family Home is an especially lovely album.

Afterwards, Sri Chinmoy clapped, and we all joined in. He was clapping not to honor himself, but rather to appreciate our receptivity to what he wanted to offer through music. We clapped thunderously for him, for proving that age is no barrier to learning and mastering a musical instrument.

Perhaps that same night Sri Chinmoy also announced that it was Sri Ramakrishna's birthday. He sold a book called "From the Undivine Tree to the Divine Fruit" about the life and spiritual journey of Girish Ghosh, a very prominent householder disciple of Sri Ramakrishna. Many years later, in 2006, some of Guru's disciples put on a play about the life of Girish Ghosh, based on this book. It was a very nice play! Sri Chinmoy said afterwards that they should have included a scene of Sri Ramakrishna blessing Girish Ghosh's actresses. But then he commented that they probably don't know enough about Girish's life to know that Sri Ramakrishna did bless many of the actresses in his troupe. He also commented that they should have included the scene where Sri Ramakrishna actually demanded that Girish drink right in front of him. Girish was ashamed of his behavior, but Sri Ramakrishna taught him that shame and embarrassment do not transform our nature. Spiritual evolution and perfection are always gradual, slow and natural.

I just remember a striking tapestry on the stage behind Sri Chinmoy. The weave depicted the famous studio portrait of Sri Ramakrishna, where he is leaning on a pillar, his hands in a particular mudra with only the pinkie and index fingers extended. I have a photograph of Sri Chinmoy playing the harmonium in front of this particular tapestry. An otherworldly smile plays on his face. You can feel his ecstatic communion with the great Avatar Sri Ramakrishna.

After the beautiful esraj concert and also after Sri Chinmoy had read out some soulful selections from his book on Girish Ghosh, he handed out prasad. It might have been some kind of Indian wrap. I just remember touching Guru's hand as he gave me the prasad. His fingers scraped against mine, and I was surprised at how hard and callused they were. They were the hands of someone who had worked hard his whole life, who had known a lot of strenuous manual labor. They were not like my soft, suburbanite hands at all.

So, it wasn't enough for Sri Chinmoy to offer us a soulful concert and a deeply devotional, thoughtful book on Sri Ramakrishna and his dear Girish. He also wanted to see us well fed. His concern for us was and remains unfathomable.

***

A HOLY STORE

In early 2000 I was taking a bus to work, some twenty miles outside of Philadelphia. I was reading one of Guru's "Seventy-Seven Thousand Service-Trees" books. A woman happened to look over my shoulder, saw what I was reading and asked me if I had acquired that book in a "holy store".

I was not familiar with the term, so I asked her what that was. She said, "Where they sell Bibles and crosses and other things."

I said, "Yes!"

BECOME RAMAKRISHNA AND THEN YOU CAN DANCE

Twice a year the Centre holds a special circus. People put on many funny skits and dress in crazy costumes. One year, maybe 2000, a lot of the silly skits involved people singing and dancing. I noticed many of the singers and dancers were untalented, but I didn't think much of it. Anyway, my favorite part of the circus is the sideshow where you can buy lots of interesting old books and tapes. Akhanka from New Hampshire sells many wonderful books from her "Sun of the Heart" bookstore. For example, I have bought two or three books on Anandamayi Ma from her. One year Guru went up to her table and leafed through a certain book on Anandamayi Ma, and then afterwards so many disciples bought copies of the book that it sold out!

Anyway, this time I did spend some time in the actual circus hall, and I saw that Guru was watching the acts with a bored, rather unhappy expression. The only act he obviously enjoyed was when a young man demonstrated his remarkable long jump ability, clearing two or three hurdles at a time. I think Guru also used to leap hurdles in his ashram days, so that gave him joy.

Anyway, the day after that particular circus, at the afternoon function, Guru just asked us to kindly not include dancing in our circus acts. He just said that it is very difficult to keep our consciousness at the highest level when we participate or observe dancing. He also wished for the acts to be less silly.

Then he said he would be happy to take questions. I remember one young man asked the Master if there was any way for us to make our dancing spiritual. I don't remember Guru's exact words, but I remember the tone and import of what he said well enough to summarize it pretty accurately. Guru just said that you may say that Lord Krishna danced and Sri Ramakrishna danced, so what is wrong with it. So, Guru continued, just become Krishna, become Ramakrishna, and then go ahead and dance. He said that if we take millions and billions of years, that will be needed for us to equal Krishna or Sri Ramakrishna in consciousness, then it will be fine for us to dance.

I am happy to say the following year's circus acts were much, much better. The French disciples did a wonderful marching routine in perfect formation to the tune of La Marseillaise. Guru obviously enjoyed it and stamped his feet to the music. The next day, after Guru gave out prasad at the afternoon function, a young German man said that, as he was watching the French march, a tear rolled down his cheek, and another one, and then before he knew it he was weeping openly. Guru asked him teasingly if he saw Napoleon.

MEDITATING AT THE GUJARATI TEMPLE ON HORACE HARDING

For part of the year in 2004, I believe Sri Chinmoy held some of our weekly meditations at a local Gujarati temple, somewhere near 175th street and Horace Harding. For various reasons we could not use PS 86 anymore so we had to find a new venue. I think Guru liked the Gujarati temple because it was very simple and very pure. It was very easy to have nice, soulful meditations there.

We would meet in the auditorium of the temple. I remember on either side of the stage there was a painting of a famous Gujarati political figure. One of the figures was Vallabh Bhai Patel, known as the "Iron Man of India" for his implacable insistence that the various, quarreling petty states join together as one united India. He persuaded all the minor Rajahs to accept and take up the cause of national unity. No mean feat! At the end of every meditation, Sri Chinmoy would circle around the room in his little "chariot" and would meditate on Vallabhbhai Patel for at least a minute. Then he would incline his head slightly and say to us," He is the Iron Man of India!"

Once after a sweet Wednesday night meditation, Sri Chinmoy was walking out of the room and pointed at the painting of Vallabhbhai Patel and said something like, "He got all the minor states under control. It's a good idea," he said, smiling, "Control yourself!"

I always preferred meditating with Sri Chinmoy in an enclosed space, whether at PS 86 or the Gujarati temple or even the tent at Aspiration-Ground. He was never fussy about where we met. You could feel the very walls of the room were different after we meditated together. They became porous, somehow, like silly putty, as if Sri Chinmoy's light had infused them with a little bit of living consciousness. His concern and love extended even to mute stone.

PART II

GEMS FROM THE INSPIRATION GROUP

MAHIRUHA KLEIN

GAVARNIE

by Sumangali Morhall.

Were I to set more store by the zodiac, I'd blame it on a Cancerian date of birth. Perhaps it has more to do with past-life experience, or maybe it's just one of those things. Either way, the fact remains: my thoughts about leaving the house generally range from ambivalence to reluctance.

I use the word house loosely, as it is neither manor nor cottage, nor even a town maisonette, but a single room by a railway line. I fancy I could live quite well somewhere as an anchoress, so long as there'd be Wi-Fi, and deliveries posted through a hatch in the wall. The only other concession might be a little patch of garden. A kettle. A heated towel rail. I wouldn't ask for much.

What could impel me then to squash bedding and four days' clothing into an improbably tiny cabin bag? What could induce me to share a room for five where mounting (and especially dismounting) a bunk will require the strangest contortions? What could draw me to the cattle-truck confines of a budget airline, not knowing where my next good cup of tea will come from?

> "Joy Days, Joy Days! Nothing gives me as much joy as Joy Days. When my children meet together to pray, meditate and play, they feed their souls, they feed their hearts, they

feed their physical existence. What else do they need?" [12]

Reaching the Pyrenees meant an overnight in Lourdes – two trains, a bus, a brief hotel, another bus, plane and cab away from my northern English home. Though life has brought me almost no experience of Christianity, I felt a kind of kinship with my fellow passengers – most of them clearly pilgrims, and in various states of health. I've waited in many an airport queue to have my tickets inspected, my bags rummaged and my person scanned for weapons. Never have I seen a queue so cheerful, so calm or polite than the one for Lourdes.

At Lourdes we would be three, and could make a small adventure between us. Although it rained prolifically, doggedly – one could almost say spitefully at times – everything but our enthusiasm was dampened. I was struck by how real and recent was the life of Saint Bernadette. I think of saints as trapped in medieval carvings or unlikely illustrations, their humanness censored and their stature extended out of all proportion. How is one then to separate miracles from the vagaries of imagination?

Like Thérèse of Lisieux, Bernadette Soubirous was alive in the late 19th Century. She has photographs. I have seen her little wooden shoe behind glass, the dress she embroidered, letters she wrote home to her brother from the convent in Nevers. I've stood inside le cachot – the dungeon – where she lived in poverty with her family at the time of the visions. I've looked on the very bed where she slept.

[12]   *Sri Chinmoy, The Temple and the Shrine, Agni Press, 2013*

While the countless gift shops are rather too gaudy and sentimental for my taste, the atmosphere at Lourdes is distinctly numinous. It also has particular qualities one might call feminine. That which is pure, gentle and nurturing is often overlooked in the West, written off as trivial or weak. I wonder, is that why God chose a simple girl of 14 to receive the visions, and specifically visions of a young Virgin Mary?

There was to be a military parade in the town that weekend, soldiers from many countries convening for services, marching the streets in elaborate uniforms, marking time with drums and shiny brass instruments. While that seemed to me rather incongruous, I suppose the chance arrival of the Peace Run seemed to them equally so! We could not light our torch, but unfurled our banner all the same, and processed to the sacred grotto for prayers and pictures.

Queuing for water in the rain may sound pointless, but it was the only way to drink from the spring that appeared at the feet of Bernadette. Families waited with us under capes and umbrellas, chattering in various languages, filling anything from their hands to glass phials and plastic gallons. Lourdes may not be an outwardly peaceful place, but inwardly, yes, and a happy place too. I was often reminded of our own gatherings in New York. Time slows down. The boundaries between people are softer than usual.

What was once a rubbish dump is now a shrine, trailed with vines and wild roses. One can pass by the edges of the cave and touch its surface. Long candles of white and blue blaze at the entrance, and thousands more wait their turn on covered tables, imbued with the prayers of those who offered them. The enormous basilica of grey stone grows as though from out of the rocks. The river Gave churns and tumbles beside it, all milky molten turquoise.

* * *

Our true destination was Gavarnie – its falls forming the source of that very river. Sri Chinmoy encouraged a special bond between our French and British Centres, and asked that we all meet four times a year for Joy Days. We may do the same things each time – meditating, singing, playing games, sharing meals, news and inspiration – but each brings a new experience.

After a languorous breakfast, most of us walked. Some of us ran. Even from the window of our gîte, I struggled to take in the scene. First there was the fat green of the ground, acres of open meadow, each blade in its Sunday best, the leaves and needles of trees outgrowing their winter jackets to stretch out bare and shiny.

But up there, where there would be sky, was an amphitheatre of limestone, dark and ruckled, draped in snow, crested in ice, coddled in cottonwool clouds. And drawn down the middle as though in dusty chalk, La Grande Cascade, the highest waterfall in all of France. Only then came the canopy of violet blue, and a very buoyant sun.

The warm air rang with birdsong. Butterflies were at their leisure, playing tag on the breezes – black, white, orange, yellow. Even ants and flies and beetles looked well fed. Bees were just as comfortably off, surveying their estates and muttering approval – blue gentians and purple orchids, too brilliant for the focus of human eyes.

The scent of pine in cool arbours. The scent of earth in sunlight. Trails were dotted with seasoned hikers and Sunday ramblers, tracking the river upstream to its source. Giant raptors wheeled above in their dozens – vultures or eagles, too high to tell. Below, each crevice spilled with melting snow and white noise. It chuckled and funnelled into pools sheer as glass, then drove recklessly on, crashing and overtaking itself, ecstatic to be free of mountain stone at last.

Whoever thought to build a hotel so high? That meant a cup of tea. A good cup of tea, and all the better for climbing. We talked of concerts, classes, other Joy Days past and yet to come. We stared into the splendour and said nothing at all – that comfortable silence enjoyed only in the best of company. The more intrepid clambered over a moonscape to the snows and the falls. Donkeys lumbered up the slope to be tethered by the grass, so their little passengers could shout and run and drink soda.

In time we ambled back to the village, ate bowls of ice cream made of local berries, and sat amongst the meadow flowers listening to cuckoos. We drove to Luz-Saint-Sauveur for galettes with native cheeses and crêpes with sweet marrons, then scrambled into our bunks to read, welcoming the sudden sleep that follows a day in mountain air.

Most left next morning with the Peace Run, and there were three of us again. We met nobody on our walk that day, save the birds, butterflies, and Notre-Dame des Neiges – Our Lady of the Snows. Her statue towers over Gavarnie, holding the child Jesus aloft as he blesses all beneath. Warmth, purity, gentleness against a rugged, icy backdrop.

All was silent but the wind across the peaks. The feminine

aspect of the divine again celebrated for its subtle yet powerful grace. Absorbed in her devotion, Notre-Dame is at once perfectly vulnerable and perfectly invulnerable. In the words of Bernadette, "One who loves does not notice her trials; or perhaps more accurately, she is able to love them."

Driving to Lourdes I realise I'm not ready to go back home. Strange for a would-be anchoress. These days have surely fed the soul, fed the heart, fed the physical existence. What else do I need?

THE GALAXY OF STARS

by Michael Howard

In a recent posting, Morris Klein mentioned a poem by Sri Chinmoy:

> There is only one sentence
> In God's entire Autobiography:
> "The galaxy of stars
> And the darkest night
> Are inseparably one."

I like what Morris and Kamalakanta said about this poem. On those rare occasions when I have been in a blissful consciousness, I've noticed that God's presence seems to announce itself in everything. It's like "Duh!, so that's what a flower means. And that was there all along?" From a higher consciousness everything seems to signify God's presence and illustrate His nature.

I remember once meditating in a park and overhearing two people engaged in ordinary conversation. Yet as I meditated more deeply, they seemed to be reciting holy words from some sacred book.

From a higher consciousness, spiritual truths seem to reveal themselves spontaneously. I had never studied Zen Buddhism very seriously, or done much work with koans, but when I was in a blissful consciousness I found myself saying "omigod, so THAT'S the sound of one hand clapping..." I remember listening to some sacred choral music and hearing only one voice – but as a kind of game, the voice had adopted many different tones, which were projections of the one Voice.

What's this got to do with the poem? You can take the night sky as a canopy for barbecues and baseball games, or as a beautiful painting. But does it have any deeper spiritual significance?

Without the galaxy of stars, the primordial darkness is like the formless and silent aspect of the Supreme, like non-existence. The galaxy of stars is like the creation bursting forth, and the billions of created souls. Even though some of these stars live for billions of years, they are only flickers on the screen of Eternity. Their life span is nothing compared to the Soul of God.

The primordial darkness and the galaxy of stars give meaning to each other. It is only by virtue of the one that we perceive the other. They are like obverse and reverse of the same coin. Together, they make up "one Truth, one Life, one Face" (to quote from Sri Chinmoy's "Invocation").

The Soul of God is not some dry philosophy, it is living and vibrant. And when we look up at the night sky, we may spontaneously perceive the vastness of this great Soul, from the fathomless depths of its silence, to the measureless heights of its creative splendour. And in the way that the stars wink at us, there is even a hint of Cosmic Humour...

In one of his plays from the collection "Siddartha Becomes The Buddha," speaking through the character of Kshema, Sri Chinmoy writes:

"Nobody can count the grains of sand on the bank of the Ganges or weigh the water in the ocean. Similarly, when you enter into Nirvana, there Bliss is infinite. It cannot be measured, weighed or counted. It is unfathomable. In that highest realm of Bliss we see the meeting place of existence and non-existence. There non-existence and existence are inseparable, indescribable." [13]

Is the night sky a kind of universal koan which, when pondered from the right consciousness, reveals to us the nature of existence and non-existence? To come full circle:

There is only one sentence
In God's entire Autobiography:
"The galaxy of stars
And the darkest night
Are inseparably one."

- Sri Chinmoy

---

[13] Sri Chinmoy, Siddhartha becomes the Buddha, Sky Publishers, New York, 1973.

MAHIRUHA KLEIN

TEARS FOR DEAD CHILDREN: AN INCIDENT FROM MALAYSIA

By Jogyata Dallas

It wasn't at all like the glossy travel brochures. On the beach in front of the Swiss Garden Hotel near Kuantan, Malaysia, the waves were a dull caramel brown, not blue, muddied by rivers swollen with silt and rain and falling on grey, not golden, sands. This dawn it was still raining and after thirty minutes of running along the hard sand the Swiss Garden had disappeared into the mist far behind me.

Even in this desolation there was a kind of beauty and you revelled in the emptiness and solitude – to be alone in this wilderness of sea, sky, endless shoreline reminds us of a truth about ourselves that is both certain and finally consoling. At the far end of my outward journey I stopped at a derelict picnic spot on an embankment above the tide – here a dilapidated table, wads of old newspaper, an abandoned wicker basket, a broken plastic chair chained absurdly to a tree. On the table an English language newspaper was smoothed out, the only deliberation in this pathos of scattered things. It was as though smoothed down by a careful hand, quite immaculate in presenting itself to my curious eyes.

And then a jolt to see there, row after row, the faces and photographs of so many dead children, laid out on the memorial pages in epitaph. Some were melancholy as though some premonition of their end had come upon them, others smiling in their best clothes and bright with life, unsuspecting and innocent of what would surely come. Beneath each the sentiments of mourning families, some touching, others platitudes dulled by convention yet all that could be said in the face of such despairing grief. And no explanation as to their sudden demise.

Sitting there in the rain, poring over each childs face, you wanted to reach out with your arms as though to protect each one from life's harshness – how it touched the heart, the neat rows of dead children, the random arbitrariness of life.

In the face of such a monumental sadness your own petty things fly away and you are left with a sense of wonder to be among the living, the consciousness-spark between the darkness at each end of physical existence.

Confronted by the portraits of the departed children you are reminded of the sacredness and brevity of your own life, that brief moment of sunlight, and you understand more clearly that each little thing you can do, or just to call out to God with an absolute sincerity, counts for something and finally measures your life's worth. Yes, each and every such moment is a powerful, redemptive thing and finally all that will remain of you.

The dead help us and remind us of what is real in our living. Beneath your wet skin you feel the slow drumbeat of your heart – your sudden tears, as much for yourself and the somber, hard mystery of human life as for the neat rows of dead children, dissolve into the rain and merge into the grass.

NEW OLD GUY

By Michael Whitebull

Hello group, I first became aware of him in the early 70's when I learned that John McLaughlin, guitarist for the Mahavishnu Orchestra, was a disciple of his. The more I learned of him, the more curious I became.

I attended a Sri Chinmoy concert in the late 80's, and fell into a trance within only a few minutes of concentrating on what Chinmoy was doing. I did not come out of it until the concert was over, and for the next several hours, I had the most overwhelming feeling of peace, love, and contentment I have ever had in my life.

Such a feeling has not occured since that time, and I have never forgotten it. When I attended another one of his concerts, I noticed many people in the audience trying to concentrate... I knew what they were trying to recreate, as I was doing the same thing, but this concert was outdoors at the Seattle Center, it was very windy, and there was a roller coaster next to the stage so concentrating was near impossible. I did not connect with him that time the way I did during the previous experience, but gave a lot of thought to becoming a disciple. The biggest problem with that is I am a terrible follower.

Chinmoy is also, IMO, one of the models used for creating the Forrest Gump character. Whatever he does, he DOES. First, it was ping pong, then it was running. They ran all over the world. Then it was weight lifting.

He performed a world record setting lift, on camera no less.

I saw him do it. Not bad for an unassuming holy man from India. No huge arms of oak, no chafing thighs, no veins popping out of his shoulders, just a modest man with a mysterious smile. I believe he does it with his mind to show us we can do anything which we set OUR minds to as well.

Chinmoy speaks of the God as a compassionate being with whom we can have a fillial relationship, which is a belief that makes me somewhat uncomfortable due to it's closeness to very many fundamentalist belief systems.

Spending 16 years practicing Nichiren Buddhism, as I have, will also shut down the "heavenly father" business pretty well. But rather than resisting the God-as-a-being concept, I have determined to try and understand it yet again, because even Jesus the Christ alludes to the same being-father-creator. These people can't be yanking our chains, they have to know something! Chinmoy often speaks at length of meeting his disciples after they die and helping them on their way. I would almost consider becoming a disciple just for the use of his celestial tow bar when this gig on earth is done.

Please forgive my overly grounded perspective; but I am a long time student of the near death experience, which has toned down many of the sentimental beliefs I picked up in younger years as a bumbling vaisnava. Like Chinmoy, many near deathers show extraordinary proof of the human/divine potential, and deserve consideration as well as anyone else who expresses unconditional love, great compassion, and unadulterated spiritual perspective. We can learn from anyone at all who has glimpsed the beyond, but Chinmoy is still one in a trillion. The Power Of Peace.

STAYING ON THE PATH

By Tejvan Pettinger

'Staying on the path' – It might not sound the most ambitious of spiritual disciplines. Perhaps many seekers will be more interested in making the fastest progress or realising God in under 2 and half years or something like that. But, for me, fully staying in Guru's boat is more than enough. When I look back at my (short) spiritual diary of significant spiritual moments; I read one account where I wrote how when I felt a deep sense of peace, I lost all desire to measure progress – even lofty goals like self-realisation seemed unimportant. It was just enough to be, knowing that being here on Guru's path was taking me somewhere beyond my wildest expectations.

To stay on the path sounds as if it is just a static goal. But, in the spiritual life there is always progress, whether it is forward or backward. If you are fully in the boat, we can make rapid progress – even if it doesn't always seem like that. Sri Chinmoy sometimes used the analogy of being on a plane. When we take off, we feel we are flying very fast, but when cruising at 500 mph, we hardly notice we are moving. Being in the boat is like cruising at altitude. Guru writes.

"There is another way to maintain your standard. It is through identification with me. Feel that I represent a boat. You have come with your ticket: regularity and aspiration. Throw yourself into the boat. There you can chant or sing or dance or sleep. You have played your part by entering into the boat. Now just stay inside the boat and the boat will carry you." [14]

However, from experience, it is only a smooth ride when you are fully in the boat. Half in and half out creates an inevitable tension; and it isn't even always obvious that we have taken the first tentative steps to stop and look around elsewhere.

One experience a friend recently related to me.

Someone in his centre was having problems with other students there. He wrote to Guru, hoping / expecting Guru would sympathise with his difficulties. Instead, the only reply he got was that they already had one foot out of the boat.

Every case is different and one should be careful about taking individual cases out of the very specific context in which they came from. But, from what I understand, if we allow the critical ego to come to the fore we are in danger of finding things wrong wherever we look; this is problematic for any spiritual path. When we think the problem is everyone else, actually the problem is invariably with our own mind.

There was a great Sufi Master, who over many years noticed a phenomena of his own disciples. Initially when they joined the path, the seekers heart's aspiration burnt intensely and the ego was sublimated or perhaps the ego would be fully immersed in trying to latch on to the spiritual progress. (giving danger of spiritual pride)

[14] Sri Chinmoy, Problems! Problems! Are they really problems? part 2, Sri Chinmoy Lighthouse, New York, 1974

But, after a few years, the initial intensity of aspiration often imperceptibly diminished, and often the ego would emerge from the shadows and come back to the fore to try and reassert itself. The ego, would start to criticise other disciples, and wonder why other people were not as spiritual. If the ego was fed and not put in its place, it's negativity could increase until it even started criticising the teacher and the path they were on. Such is the path of criticism and negativity – once we see negativity in one place, before we know it, we will see it in the whole world.

To stay on the path, we need to value the path of the heart. The heart which is tolerant, non-judgemental and self-giving. Taking this positive, optimistic approach to life is an essential component of the spiritual life.

What other qualities do we need to stay on the path?

The first thing is to be happy. If we are happy, everything is easier. But happiness doesn't come just from pleasing yourself. The greatest happiness comes when we can be genuinely self-giving, and seek to give something to others. It is important not just to be a consumer 'what can I get' but 'What can I give' – It is giving back something that gives a sense of value, and this is important.

One thing Guru always encouraged us to do is to give meditation classes. Not so much to find new seekers but because it is one of the best things for our own spiritual life. When we can offer something to fellow seekers, it is one of the strongest ways to strengthen our own spiritual life; they say 90% of learning is in teaching. When giving talks / classes on meditation – we remember how to meditate ourself, we remember how much value there is in the spiritual life.

***

Turning up

I sometimes joke to myself that the spiritual life is 90% about turning up. When we spend time in the boat, we gain the benefits of being there. But, if we devote more time to the myriad attractions of the world, then our focus changes, and we lose that connection to spirituality.

The great spiritual Master, Sri Ramakrishna said the human mind was like blotting paper; it absorbs whatever it is exposed to. If we spend time with spiritual aspirants, we subconsciously absorb this spiritual energy. If we spend time reading the newspaper or some internet forum, we absorb that consciousness – even if we think we are rejecting it, it does imperceptibly seep in.

Fortunately, the modern spiritual life of Sri Chinmoy is comparatively easy. In the ancient days, spirituality was perhaps meditating into the early hours of the morning. But, for us, spirituality also involves singing, running or just turning up for 'joy days' – a weekend of having a good time.

I have always come back from a joy weekend more appreciative of the spiritual path I'm on. Even if you don't feel like travelling a long way to a joy day, you know it is worth the effort because that intensity of being in a spiritual energy is a very easy way to strengthen the commitment to the spiritual life.

***

Remembering the good experiences

"If I had to define man it would be: a biped, ungrateful."
Fyodor Dostoevsky

Perhaps, this quote from Dostoevsky is true. But perhaps it just that we are very good at forgetting, especially forgetting the uplifting, spiritual experiences we have had.

No matter who you are, be it Swami Vivekananda or very much a beginner seeker, there is no one who hasn't had dry periods in the spiritual life; but it is equally true that no seeker hasn't had good experiences. But these memorable experiences can also be easily forgotten, dwarfed by our temporary difficulties. Re-reading our past experiences can bring them back into our mind, and remind us why we have been following the spiritual life for so long. We may begin with imagination, but imagination can definitely be a precursor to reality.

Perhaps the problem is that the loftiest experiences can be so far removed from the mundane drama of the world, that we can even doubt whether we went so high. One note I re-read from many years ago – when I was meditating well, it felt like I had woken from a dream, and was fully awake from the first time. I wish I could experience this at will, alas I can't. But, I will always keep the memory of that experience alive because I know *nothing* will ever be able to give that same satisfaction and intensity of joy.

My spiritual diary used to be very short and infrequent – perhaps because I was waiting for an experience of nirvana before I would take pen to paper. But, now, I'm less fussy. If you have an experience of genuine satisfaction, real happiness – or the ability to get out of a bad mood and replace it with something better – is this not a miracle worthy of inclusion?

***

Just try for one incarnation

I do believe in reincarnation. You don't need to believe in reincarnation to meditate, but it does help with the spiritual life. I remember one very strong, intense talk Guru gave about the spiritual life. Amongst many other things, Guru said something like: 'For so many incarnations you have tried pleasing yourself. Can you not just for one incarnation try to lead a genuine spiritual life and see where it takes you? If you feel you are missing out on worldly experiences, definitely you will be able to have them in some future incarnation. But for this incarnation be sincere to your spiritual life.

William Shakespeare said:

"This above all: to thine own self be true, And it must follow, as the night the day, Thou canst not then be false to any man."

If I am really honest with myself, it is the spiritual quest that I really want. No trinkets of the world can compare.

One of the hardest things in the spiritual life is to be honest with yourself. Understanding your real motivation and sincerity behind actions and even thoughts.

We have to ask ourselves? Are we really listening to the promptings of our soul or is the part of us (mind / vital) which seeks outer recognition and outer pleasure? It is said that is easy to deceive others. But, if we deceive ourselves, the spiritual life is very shallow. Sometimes I catch myself trying to justify an action. But, if I'm really honest with myself this action is not being true to the path of the heart, the path of the soul. Sometimes it feels like progress just to stop justifying why you are doing something wrong. There is a certain humility in knowing why you are doing something. It's important not to be too hard on yourself, but we need to always be honest, and retain the aspiration to aim for something higher.

It is no shame in being at a low standard (whatever a low standard is), as long as we keep aiming to improve our standard. There was a great disciple of Sri Ramakrishna (Girish Chandra Ghosh) he led an undivine life to stay the least. He couldn't see how he could transform his life. Sri Ramakrishna just told him to always keep in mind his Master, whatever he did. Eventually, this remembrance of his Master and the ideals of the spiritual life would bring his conscience and soul to the fore. Girish did eventually make the most radical transformation due to his devotion to his Master. The important thing is to never give up and accept our standard as unchangeable. Simply valuing the spiritual life and the aspiration to aim for something higher is very important.

When we really follow the spiritual life, there is a sense of satisfaction, and we lose that inner tension, that inner conflict. Because when we are following the path, there is a strong inner harmony – even if the outer world is not as reliable.

Staying on the path is the easiest and hardest thing all at once. When we are 100% in the boat, we know there is nothing more you could want. But, it is equally easy to slip into the gossip world or judgement world. When we start looking all around us, we can start to doubt our own spirituality and imperceptibly slip away from the spiritual life.

I agree 100% with Ramakrishna that my mind is just like blotting paper, I guess we just need to keep dipping it in the right ink.

I don't want much in this life, but I do want to stay on the path until the very end.

DEFINING MOMENTS

By Sharani Robbins

When someone enters into the circle dance with God, a dictionary of defining moments unfolds. The seeker experiences some defining moment that opens up the very existence of God into his/her life. Sri Chinmoy uses a vivid image of words and realities being written in gold letters on the tablet of our hearts. Thus, I imagine this dictionary resides in our spiritual hearts. Inner experiences, moments of spiritual union and sweet lessons build one upon another into defining moments of our existence.

This afternoon a palette of light, clouds and even a few random acts of snowflakes strode past my window. If I turned from my work, each view out of the window brought a different play of sun, clouds and sky. I was lost in a reverie of Monet's haystacks and the notion that I could happily spend hours just watching how the progressing light of the day paints masterpiece after masterpiece – all for free!

At one moment, the sun was mostly shining yet something barely perceptible was falling from the sky. I looked more closely and some very light snow was falling. I was off to test the theory of whether or not sun and snow could create rainbows. I think not but the sky was alive with blue, pink, grey, mauve, white and black.

The flakes of snow were so infrequent that one doubted their true existence. Acts of mercy and goodness from others and

God perhaps suffer the same fate as they are overshadowed by the ubiquitous suffering and injustice in the world.

But both are true regardless of their sometimes faint expression. And they led me to ponder defining moments of who God is for each and every traveler on pilgrimage to divinity. One time Sri Chinmoy said {unofficial}

"My name is my Lord's Forgiveness" and in the endless expressions of unconditional forgiveness, which for me is perhaps the greatest defining reality of God, then I felt this word is more my name than even the spiritual name given to me by Sri Chinmoy. For my journey could not even exist without that initial spark of forgiveness that offers the biggest bum business deal of all time from God's point of view. God's Light and Love in exchange for my hurt, fear and all other varieties of ignorance. Even the seed of an inner cry hid from me for years and I fall down as often as I walk forward. Therefore, I would probably choose the word forgiveness if asked to define who and what God is.

What are your defining moments? I'm sure that just as we have completely unique fingerprints our definitions of God would likely straddle the vastness and universality that He/She encompasses.

Now the sun sets. Even though these moments pass in a fleeting instant, I hope we can memorize them at least inside the tablet of our hearts and tell their stories to every soul hungry for divinity.

ABOUT THE AUTHOR

Mahiruha Klein was born 1 November 1975 in the United States. Incidently on that very same date, Sri Chinmoy wrote his record-breaking poetry book *Transcendence-Perfection* – 843 poems composed in a 24 hour period.

Mahiruha has been a disciple of Sri Chinmoy since 1997. He currently resides in Chicago, where he works in a Whole Food store.

On different occassions he has memorised whole sets of Sri Chinmoy's poetry books, including *Transcendence-Perfection, The Wings of Light, The Dance of Light* and *The Golden Boat*. The last three poetry series each contain 1,000 poems each and their recital took several hours. A recent recital of *The Wings of Light* was given at Oneness-Heart Centre in Jamaica, New York, 2022. Several people who attended were so moved, they stayed for several hours because of the profound experience of Sri Chinmoy's poetry and consciousness.

Vilas Silverton – Cover Artist

Vilas is a visionary artist, who lives in Bristol. He is also a student of Sri Chinmoy, who has completed several long-distance cycling challenges, including the Indian Pacific Wheel Race across Australia.

www.ingramcontent.com/pod-product-compliance
Lightning Source LLC
Chambersburg PA
CBHW021153080526
44588CB00008B/312